MARKETING
for
Financial
Advisors

MARKETING

— *for* —

Financial
Advisors

*Build Your Business, Bring in Clients,
and Establish Your Brand*

ERIC T. BRADLOW

KEITH E. NIEDERMEIER   PATTI WILLIAMS

New York   Chicago   San Francisco   Lisbon   London
Madrid   Mexico City   Milan   New Delhi   San Juan
Seoul   Singapore   Sydney   Toronto

ISBN: 978–0–07–160514–4
MHID: 0–07–160514–2

This publication is designed to provide accurate and authoritative information in regard to the subject matter covered. It is sold with the understanding that the publisher is not engaged in rendering legal, accounting, or other professional service. If legal advice or other expert assistance is required, the services of a competent professional person should be sought.

—From a declaration of principles jointly adopted by a committee of the American Bar Association and a committee of publishers.

McGraw-Hill books are available at special quantity discounts to use as premiums and sales promotions, or for use in corporate training programs. To contact a representative, please visit the Contact Us pages at www .mhprofessional.com.

Eric Bradlow dedicates this book to Laura, Ethan, Zachary, and Benjamin

Keith Niedermeier dedicates this book to Michelle, Andy, and Brian

Patti Williams dedicates this book to Dylan, Evie, and Calder

CONTENTS

PREFACE
Is It Time to Attack
or to Retreat?

At the time we are writing this book, the world is faced with unparalleled economic challenges not seen since the Great Depression. Firms, especially in the financial services industry, are going out of business, people are unemployed, and even the most fortunate of firms are tightening their belts. Simply put, rough economic seas require a good captain to navigate through tough choices. Even when things are going well, targeting, segmentation, and branding, all topics that are described in detail in this book, often do not receive the attention they deserve. When times are tough, these topics typically get even less attention. Marketing academics commonly joke that the field of marketing is cyclical. When things are going well, marketing generates revenue; when things are down, marketing is a cost center to be reduced. Many managers might say, "Is this the time for marketing? Marketing is a cost. We are cutting costs. To stay competitive, we have to cut costs."

This mindset is unfortunately both commonplace and misguided. We do not mean to say that cost cutting where appropriate is a bad idea. Rather, in this book we emphasize a data-oriented way to assess the return on investment (ROI) of your marketing spending and hence how to think about optimizing that investment. Cut the marketing costs that are not delivering for your business, but maintain or even increase spending on investments that are yielding returns. In this book, we will argue that you often have to trade off short-run profitability to invest in your brand and your customers for the long haul. Thus, efficiency depends on your time perspective. For example, in today's world of social networks, blogs, and so on, does a customer have to be a heavy buyer to be valuable to your firm? Given the ease of networking and information diffusion, a client with low investable assets could be of high strategic importance. Thus, cutting investments in marketing to these important clients could have a long-term negative effect. Simply put, marketing is not just a cost. Investments made in marketing, even in the worst of economic times, can yield dividends for your practice.

Marketing your financial services practice may require funds (e.g., for pamphlets, an improved Web site, and other such materials). Marketing your financial services firm takes time, and your time is costly and valuable. However, marketing should not be viewed as a cost to be minimized, but rather as a key driver of revenue. Marketing is perhaps the primary driver of new revenue for your practice. Ultimately, you are investing in your business for profits, and at the end of the day, profits = revenues − costs. The purpose of this book is to help you, the financial advisor, improve the

profitability of your practice. Our experience has shown that
this is most easily accomplished through building the customer relationships you want by targeting the appropriate
segments and clients, which when combined, leads to profitability. Marketing is the engine driving that profitability
through revenue enhancement.

This leads to the question postulated in the title of this
preface: Is it time to attack or to retreat? Let us consider the
following framework that will help us answer that question.

IS IT TIME TO ATTACK OR TO RETREAT?

Any marketer who claims to "know" whether to increase
investment (broadly defined as time, money, effort, and so
on) in marketing during difficult economic times (attack) or
to save one's cash flow for better economic times (retreat)
is probably stretching the believability of the word *know*.
However, there is a well-established marketing framework
that can offer some guidance:

$$\text{Market share} = f(\text{share of voice} \times \text{share of distribution} \times \text{share of preference})$$

What does this equation mean to you in the financial services industry? There are three main components involved
in obtaining your share of the financial services market (see
Figure P.1). First comes share of voice. Stated another way,
this is the share of marketing communications that your
practice obtains relative to that obtained by other practices

Figure P.I The Three Scales of Market Share

Share of Voice   Share of Distribution   Share of Preference

in your competition set. For instance, imagine a market with four firms where the expenditures of the firms directed toward a given local market segment are $50,000, $30,000, $15,000, and $5,000, respectively. Thus, Firm 1's share of voice is $50,000/($50,000 + $30,000 + $15,000 + $5,000) = 50 percent. Assuming that distribution and preference are equal, then, Firm 1 will get approximately 50 percent of the market. This, of course, assumes that marketing awareness ("voice") is proportional to current spending, which may be a rough approximation in mature markets where firms have entrenched awareness. In any event, share of voice (share of relevant spending) is important to know.

What is the implication of this in a recessionary market? Imagine that you are Firm 1 and that you could increase your expenditures to $100,000, but your competitors cannot. Perhaps because of bad economic times, they may even have to cut their expenditures. All of a sudden your share of voice is $100,000/$150,000 = 66.7 percent. Depending on the market size, this might be a very large win scenario for your firm. Furthermore, if your expenditures grow the market for the other firms by bringing in enough people who previously were nonclients to compensate for their loss of share, they may not retaliate against your spending increase. This is the classic "attack" scenario. That is, not only can you increase your share of voice as a result of your budgetary capability, but your competition may even be thankful if you can also grow the pie.

Let us contrast this to more robust economic times is where you might also double your expenditures to $100,000. Because all of your competitors may also be doing well in good economic times, they might also double their expenditures. Now, your share of voice is $100,000/$200,000 = 50 percent, the same as before. The big difference is that your ROI on your advertising spending is lower, as it took you $100,000 to get a 50 percent share of voice as compared to just $50,000 before. This is a classic "prisoner's dilemma" problem of the sort that we discuss in Chapter 1, where you and your competitors have an incentive to increase your expenditures as long as everyone doesn't do it. However, since each financial advisor has the incentive to increase spending, most do, and average profit for the industry is lower. Thus, many smart firms see down economic times as a better opportunity than good economic times.

Returning to the three scales of market share, let us now consider share of distribution. Share of distribution (in a conventional marketing channel, say for a consumer packaged good) is the fraction of retail outlets in which your product is available relative to the fraction in which your competition is available. The analogy for distribution in the financial services industry, which we discuss throughout the book, is getting into the consideration set of your potential clients. That is, imagine that you are targeting lawyers in your geographical area who make over $250,000 per year. If this target segment has a population of 1,000, suppose that 500 of them know you. Therefore, you are available, or potentially distributed, to 500 lawyers. What would it take to be in the consideration set for 700 instead of 500? As with the share of voice example, in down economic times, there is an opportunity to become strongly considered by major clients because one's competition may not have adequate resources to do the same. Furthermore, share of distribution is considered by most to be a very enduring form of competitive advantage, as once you have a given set of clients locked up, or once a given set of clients knows you and considers you, these clients will "always" do so.

Last, but not least, there is share of preference. Share of preference refers to how much you are "preferred" relative to competitive practices. Note that we have put preferred in quotes because there are many aspects of brand and firm preference that we discuss throughout the book. This should not be seen as meaning simply "liking," as there are many dimensions, such as trust, friendship, loyalty, and admiration, that all contribute to the preference landscape. Clearly, your firm wants to have all of these aspects associated with it, and each is part of your brand. However, just as with share of voice and share of preference, it is relative standing that matters.

With this framework in mind, the questions you should ask are:

Which of the three scales is my weakest link?

How do I know which one to improve first?

While the answer to the first question may seem to imply the answer to the second question, that may not be the right strategy for you and your financial services practice. Let us address each of these questions in turn.

Which of the three scales, share of voice, share of distribution, and share of preference, is the weakest link? The best way to assess this is data based. In particular, a financial services practice should understand its awareness compared to its competitors by surveying its customers. It should understand how seriously it is considered by its top potential clients. This information could be collected by surveys or by one-on-one interviews. Finally, a financial services practice should understand what aspects of its service clients prefer, and which require improvement. This is not information that a practice should collect once and then forget about. Rather, each practice should collect this information continuously, maintaining a current understanding of where things stand. As we describe in Chapter 7, this is the "triage" of marketing—what is the cause of dollar assets under management not being at the desired level, or if it is where you want it to be, how can you improve it?

Which one of share of voice, share of distribution, or share of preference should be improved first?

While the common intuition is to fix the one where you are the lowest, the appropriate answer is to "invest" in the one where your ROI will be the greatest. Whether it is in terms of dollars or in terms of time, which one will improve the most from the extra expenditure? To assess this, a seminal marketing paper on an approach called decision calculus[1] was written. In this approach, one takes the following steps:

1. Assemble a panel of 10 or so experts (peers, people who understand your firm, and so on).

2. Ask each individual in the panel to independently answer the following five questions about XXX = {share of voice, share of distribution, or share of preference}, where XXX is one of these three aspects of market share forecasting that you are trying to measure via the decision calculus approach:

Q1. What is your current share of XXX?

Q2. What would your share of XXX be if you were to increase spending on it by 50 percent?

Q3. What would your share of XXX be if you were to increase spending on it by 100 percent?

Q4. What would your share of XXX be if you were to decrease spending on it by 50 percent?

Q5. What is the maximum level of XXX that you could achieve if you were to spend the highest possible amount on XXX?

3. Average these answers separately across the (10-person) panel for each of the five questions and each value of XXX to get a single set of numbers (i.e., five numbers each for share of awareness, distribution, and preference).

4. Based on this information, allocate resources to that aspect that is expected to give you the greatest ROI.

As an example, consider the two curves in Figure P.2, where the curve with the diamonds corresponds to share of voice (SOV) and the curve with the rectangles corresponds to share of distribution (SOD).

As we can see, the firm is currently at about 30 percent for both SOD and SOV, and the greatest improvement would

Figure P.2 Decision Calculus: Your Way to Profitability

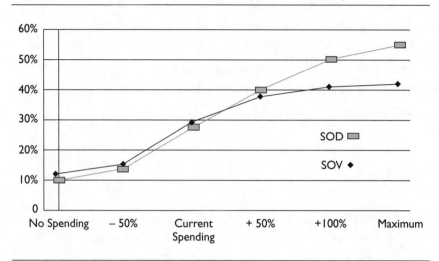

come from increasing expenditures on SOD, as the gain is greater for SOD than for SOV.

This approach has many benefits, including using your financial services partners and experts to aid your business, forcing you and your partners to think about the return on spending, and helping financial services practices understand their weakest link.

SUMMARY: ATTACK OR RETREAT?

So, what should you and your practice do today? Assuming that you can afford it, most likely the answer is "attack." Although your natural tendency may be to cut costs and avoid risky expenditures, this is exactly the time when the ROI from expenditures is likely to be the highest. This is a time when the competition is least likely to respond. This is a time when potential clients are anxious and feel that they need expertise. This book will give you a complete arsenal for structuring your attack: how to think strategically about your practice, which clients to target, and a set of methods to understand how to build truly profitable relationships with them.

NOTES

1 Leonard M. Lodish, Ellen Curtis, Michael Ness, and M. Kerry Simpson, "Sales Force Sizing and Deployment Using a Decision Calculus Model at Syntex Laboratories," *Interfaces* 18, no. 1 (January-February 1988), 5–20.

MARKETING
for
Financial
Advisors

CHAPTER 1

TREATING YOUR FINANCIAL PRACTICE LIKE A SMALL BUSINESS

INTRODUCTION: A SERVICE ORIENTATION

Our experience as academics and our years of teaching people about marketing in the financial services industry have taught us that one fact *always* holds:

Start treating your practice like a small business or you will be out of business.

This book is intended to help you move from a sales orientation to an entrepreneurial orientation. Marketing is critical to every entrepreneur. To state it in a more provocative way:

If you don't have time to make marketing critical to your practice, just wait—you soon will.

Those financial advisors (FAs) who want to succeed need to recognize that the financial services industry is just that: a service industry. We have personally conducted surveys of over 800 financial advisors from the top financial firms from around the world,[1] and recent surveys from the "World Wealth Report 2008"[2] and other major research firms corroborate the importance of service. Over and over again, customer service and understanding the needs of one's clients shows up as the number one driver of success; delivering high or above-average financial returns to your clients is listed as fourth.

When we state that a marketing orientation is a must, we are not just relying on third-party sources. Through a carefully designed survey that we have conducted over the last five years, we are bringing your voice, the voice of the financial advisor, to the development of a set of best practices. That is, by collecting and analyzing your survey responses with well-established principles of marketing, we are able to provide a detailed set of strategic suggestions and tactics that can improve an FA's business. There is no better source of field research to determine what has worked and what has not than FAs themselves. This is the unique value proposition of this book that separates it from others that are much less data-oriented.

This book, however, is not just for the "winners." It would be silly to imagine that only successful financial advisors have that "secret formula." Thus, we have surveyed financial advisors at all stages of their career. This includes those who are just starting out and trying to build their practices, a time when customer acquisition may be of central importance. We have surveyed individuals and taught executive education courses to clients in that elite group with more than $100 million in total assets under management who focus all of their efforts on ultra-high-net-worth clients (more than $5 million). We have surveyed individuals who have built their practices and now primarily want to maintain their customer base, so that customer retention is of central importance.

Our data and this book also apply to branch managers and those who are looking to brand the various financial services teams that work in their branch offices. It also applies to those assistants and support people at financial services firms who want to understand the role that they can play in making their designated financial consultant or office a success. These valuable men and women act as the gatekeepers for all interactions between clients and the firm and are the first contact a client has with an FA's practice.

The overwhelming importance of a marketing orientation rather than a high-return orientation may seem like heresy and, further, impossible to believe. In fact, a customer-centric view of your practice will provide you, as we will describe throughout this book, with the ability to achieve all the ultimate goals you desire. That is, a high book value under management does not just happen. Acquisition of high-net-worth clients does not just happen. In fact, data suggest that it takes 1.5 years, on average, to acquire a single high-net-worth client. Reaching elite status in your firm does not just happen. It is the small and meaningful *intermediate* goals along the way that make it happen. It is these intermediate goals that we lay out that will provide you with a summary marketing plan for success.

Using marketing lingo, we would identify some of these intermediate goals (and we have sections on each of these throughout the book) as:

- *Developing a value proposition.* What unique product or service does your financial advisory practice provide in comparison to others? What is your point of differentiation?

- *Developing that successful initial point of contact.*
  Do you have that 15-second "elevator speech" that tells
  prospective clients what unique services you provide?
  In other words, many financial advisors ignore or at
  least invest too little time in the communication aspects
  of their job.
- *Developing your "three words."* Most individuals will
  remember at most three basic messages when you
  introduce yourself to them. What would you like those
  to be, for you?
- *Developing your "word-of-mouth army."* It is no secret
  that the financial advice business is driven by referrals.
  Now that you have your value proposition and your
  three words, whom would you like to have talking about
  you, especially in your local community?
- *Developing a deep understanding of your clients.*
  A fundamental understanding of your clients' decision-
  making processes and psychology will aid you in acquiring
  new clients and satisfying the ones you already have. We
  will give you insights that will help you get a bigger wallet
  share, create loyalty, and encourage referrals.
- *Developing a niche segment.* What target set of clients
  are you going after? If your answer is "all of them,"
  then (only somewhat facetiously) you desperately
  need this book. We will make the case that you have
  a competitive advantage in acquisition when you are
  focused on a subset of clients. There are also those
  clients whose acquisition cost clearly outstrips their
  value. These clients must not be acquired, and if you
  have them, you need to fire them. Or, even better, as we
  will describe, let them fire themselves.

- *Developing your positioning statement.* Simply put, out of all the choices clients have for selecting a financial advisor, why you? What is so special about you? We have found that many financial advisors, when cold-called in class, asked to think about this in a survey, or asked to state it in a mock initial client meeting, have a very difficult time stating what they bring that is unique. If you cannot clearly and quickly communicate why someone should invest with you, how can you expect your clients to do it when they refer you to others?

- *Bringing it all together in a marketing plan.* With a value statement, target segment, and positioning statement in mind, how tactically will you achieve your objectives? A marketing plan helps clarify things for you, your clients, your partners, and your staff.

While this might initially seem overwhelming, our intention in this book is to take you through these steps one by one, with the goal that by the end you will be able to construct a marketing plan that is tailored to you. In addition, we will provide you with an outline for a marketing plan that can act as your guide. Now those readers who are familiar with full-service and elaborate marketing plans might, and rightly should, be thinking, doesn't developing a marketing plan take months and cost hundreds of thousands of dollars or more to employ a firm to do it, and isn't the plan usually hundreds of pages long? The answer is typically yes, yes, and yes. While we would never (and appropriately so) recommend that a practice not do this, the goal of this book is quite different. Here, the goal we are talking about is a "one-page" marketing plan. This is not to say that everything can be contained in this one page; however, our experience has shown that one can distill the key strategic and tactical elements into a very small amount of space. Furthermore, the development of a plan that is not as daunting increases with its simplicity, as does the likelihood of its not just sitting on your desk as a useless paperweight. This book is a guide to turning your financial services practice into a marketing-oriented business, one step at a time.

We will start this path with the most central organizing concept in marketing, your five Cs and four Ps. We will talk about each of these briefly in general terms (as a generic marketing course would) and then discuss them specifically as they play a role in the financial services industry.

THE FIVE Cs AND THEIR APPLICATION TO YOUR FINANCIAL SERVICES PRACTICE

Before any financial advisor tries to enact positive change, he must take stock of his current situation. It is sometimes useful to think of this through the analogy of a patient walking into an emergency room with a malady (in your case, assets under management that do not reach your objectives) and the doctor triaging (taking stock of) that patient to determine the cause. Examples in the financial services industry can be wide ranging, including poor performance in making initial contacts, converting contacts to leads, converting leads to clients, retention of clients, getting a large dollar wallet share from your clients, and so on. It is exactly this causal analysis for which the five Cs and four Ps framework was developed.

To the untrained, taking stock may lead to either pages and pages of text that are useless at the end because of their lack of structure or loads of spreadsheets that try to capture every micro facet of a business but miss the big picture. Fortunately, the tools that marketing scholars have developed for years[3] to organize information into the five Cs and four Ps of any business situation are directly applicable to your financial services practice. Thus, to avoid losing the big picture here, we will lay out these principles one at a time, and with each principle provide sample answers to these questions based on the survey data that we have collected. Our hope is that after reading this chapter, you will find a place in your one-page marketing plan for writing down your five Cs and four Ps.

The basic five Cs of any business can be summarized by an assessment of your:

1. Customers (clients)
2. Company
3. Competition
4. Context
5. Collaborators

Each of these plays an integral role in your practice, and ignoring any one of the five can lead to suboptimal performance.

Clients

The first C is where your financial services practice begins, continues, and ends: your clients. It would be trite to say,

"Pay attention to your clients!" and that is not what this C is about. Rather, how many financial advisors have taken a systematic and quantitative look at their clients? Do you have the correct mix of clients? Do you have too many clients? That is possible. In fact, our survey data suggest that the average financial advisor should have no more than 75 to 100 major clients at any one time [we will expand on this later when we talk about client relationship management (CRM) in Chapter 7]. Does each of your clients provide positive net present value (NPV)—that is, financial returns—to your practice, and how do you know this? Which of your clients have strategic value and may be able to act as the aforementioned word-of-mouth ambassadors? While this may be a cold way to look at things, each and every client must be scored on a number of dimensions. This book will lay out those dimensions and provide you the means with which to compute your client "scorecard."

Furthermore, do you understand the reasons that your clients chose you in the first place, the reasons they stay with you (or leave), and the reasons they refer you? Chapter 5 delves deeply into the client decision-making process to help you gain insights into what drives prospects to choose you and clients to stay with you. However, you know that clients do not always act rationally. Chapter 6 dives deeper into investor psychology to illuminate the underlying reasons for the strange and sometimes frustrating things that clients do or refuse to do. You will increase your value to your clients if you understand them better and help them make better and more optimal decisions. Lastly, Chapter 9 will give you specific approaches (tactics) to collecting client information that will help you formulate your marketing strategy.

Company

If you are taking an entrepreneurial approach and trying to build your business for the long term, then we must define the company as *you*. There is a growing trend for advisors to become independent. If this is your situation, then you absolutely must treat your practice as a service-based business that you are managing for the long haul. You may also be part of a team or a partnership or have your own small firm, in which case you would define this as the company. Even if you are an employee or closely affiliated with a large financial services company, you should be focused on building *your* business. Being affiliated with a large corporation has its advantages, but it does not allow you to ignore the long-term impact of marketing. The ultimate responsibility for your portfolio of clients and your future rests with you!

One of the primary tools used to form your marketing strategy is a SWOT analysis. This is an exercise in which you identify the *s*trengths, *w*eaknesses, *o*pportunities, and *t*hreats to your company. This exercise is widely used by companies both large and small (this is described more fully in Chapter 2). Strengths and weaknesses are of critical importance because, as we will explain throughout the book, it is critical that you create a match between your strengths and a specific niche of clients. While strengths and weaknesses are internal factors that clearly fall under the company C, opportunities and threats are concerned with external factors, which can include elements of the competition, customers, and context Cs. No matter how you categorize it, the goal is to create a marketing strategy that leverages your strengths, mitigates your weaknesses, capitalizes on your opportunities, and diminishes your threats.

This starts with a critical look at yourself. Research on your current clients, as we describe in Chapter 9, will help you implement your SWOT analysis.

In the financial services industry, a firm's reputation is one of its greatest strengths or potentially greatest weaknesses. Financial products are increasingly viewed as commodities. Prospects and clients are not so much making decisions based on the products that you offer, but rather on your reputation for service and advice. This can be manifested in different ways, but what we are really talking about is your *brand*. The world's best companies, like Coca-Cola or Procter & Gamble, treat their brands as assets. They invest in them, build them, and protect them. You should, too. Building and managing your reputation, or brand, is imperative to your success as an advisor. Chapter 4 will spell out the critical elements of good branding and take you through the steps needed for building yours. We will help you identify your core competency and value proposition and, just as importantly, how to communicate them effectively.

Competition

When marketers try to understand the role that competition plays in their business, it usually comes down to one central question: is it a zero-sum game or not? Consider that there are a number of basic ways for you to increase your revenues: (1) raise prices (e.g., fees), (2) increase your client base (i.e., customer acquisition), and (3) increase your dollar wallet share from your current clients. But the question is, how are you going to do that? If one assumes (and in the financial services industry this is a fair assumption) that the number of "attractive" clients and the "total wealth to be managed" is a fairly fixed-size pie, then if you gain, someone else loses. This changes the nature of competition dramatically. Contrast this with a situation in which, because of your own marketing efforts, a lot of nonusers of a given product now buy (this is called category expansion). Then, in fact, your competition may be quite happy that you are advertising your services, since even though their market share might decline (temporarily), it will easily be offset by the growth in the market.

While it is possible that through your efforts you will be able to shift some investors who do not use advisors to doing so (move them from self-managed to managed), it is less likely, and their acquisition costs are likely to be much higher. Thus, competition will clearly play a significant role in the strategy of your practice. A bigger question, however, is, "Who is your real competition?" It does not include every financial advisor in your area. This is too large a set and fails to recognize brand tiers. For instance, someone from a small firm is unlikely to try to attract or have the ability to attract the same clients as someone who works at a large, prominent firm. This is good for both parties! Furthermore, a financial advisory typically has or should have a focus, e.g., retirement planning. This is the basis of segmentation and is a primary tenet of the marketing approach and this book.

So, how do you collect information on who your competitors are? We recommend the following tactics, all of which can be implemented fairly easily and should be part of your larger interest in a data-oriented/driven practice.

- *Ask your prospects.* It is not unreasonable to ask your prospective clients what other advisory firms they are considering or which they have used in the past. This is a great source of information, and questions like these, which fall under the rubric of "unaided awareness and consideration," are strong predictors of eventual choice. Although it is possible to get into someone's unaided awareness set through various forms of advertising, not being in someone's set at the time the choice is made guarantees that you will not be selected. Furthermore, if you are in someone's set only at the time of choice, as opposed to prior to choice, this reduces the odds of your attaining that person's business in the first place. Wouldn't it be informative to know whether you did not get someone's business because he knew about you, considered you, and didn't select you or because he didn't know about you and hence couldn't select you? One (the former) is an image problem, and the other (the latter) is an awareness problem. Although we will discuss this later in the book, given a choice, take the latter problem.

- *Ask the churning clients.* Departing customers are an excellent source of information for any firm. Firms that want to continuously improve should hold exit interviews to understand where their ex-clients are going, the reasons for their departure, and whether they are likely to be a source of negative word of mouth. That is, part of customer relationship management is to "lose customers the good way." We will discuss this in Chapter 7.

- *Ask your board of advisors.* You may be saying to yourself, "Who is that? I don't have a board of advisors." Well, you should. One of the dominant themes we have heard from the hundreds of financial advisors we have taught is the value of a set of trusted opinions. While this is discussed in Chapter 9, you need to know that there are sources within your local community that can easily help you ascertain your competitive set.

Context

Context refers to the general situation the firm faces at the current time. For instance, what is the economic climate? Are you currently gaining or losing clients? Have you recently had a negative word-of-mouth event, or just the opposite, a great opportunity to brand yourself? The reason why the context is so important to one's strategy is that it provides a set of real-world constraints. To bring this C to life, consider the following vignettes.

Example 1: Out of Time, Out of Money, and Out of Business

William is a highly successful financial advisor. He determines that a good long-run strategy for him is to focus his efforts on high-net-worth clients, as he has been good at acquiring and retaining them. On the surface, this is a good plan for him. However, William is forgetting the context, which is that the economy is in decline, he is losing clients, and the confidence that his community has in him is waning. Thus, *if* he still has an active and vibrant practice in two years, then his strategy might be successful. However, current projections suggest that because of the context, he will never be able to reap the benefits. William decides instead to focus on making sure that he retains his current clients and trying to get a larger dollar wallet share of their assets under management because this is a good short- to medium-term strategy.

Example 2: Wrong Time to Advertise

Liz, as a data-oriented financial advisor, has determined that she has an awareness problem. She is tremendous at closing the deal, but many potentially attractive clients just don't know who she is. Liz determines that she will launch a media campaign to raise awareness, generate leads, and hopefully improve her client base. All of this sounds good on the surface. Unfortunately, Liz's corporate firm, not her local branch, has recently suffered some public relations issues, and by advertising, she will just bring even greater visibility and salience to these issues in the consumers' minds. Recognizing this, Liz decides to spend the time she has allocated to marketing efforts to damage control and uses direct client contact, namely meetings, and her word-of-mouth army to bring a positive image to her practice prior to advertising.

Example 3: The Wrong Segment

Ron is a financial advisor with a strong marketing orientation who has decided to refocus his efforts on a target segment that he has never worked with before: physicians. As this is a target market that has significant stored wealth and has a lot in common, especially temperamentwise, with Ron, he is confident that he will have a good rapport with it. On the surface, this is a good plan for Ron. However, Ron is overlooking the competition and has failed to recognize that a different financial advisor in his region also has an MD degree. Whenever the two of them go head-to-head for clients, the other financial advisor is more credible. After his first few attempts, Ron quickly realizes this and changes the focus of his segmentation strategy, as he determines that physicians are not a winnable segment.

Collaborators

"Win-win." If all of us had a dollar for every time we have heard this, we would be wealthy. Despite being a catchy slogan, however, this does embody the collaborators C. Simply put, who else has to "win" if you are to win? This is something that is commonly overlooked in a financial services practice, as many financial advisors see themselves as the sole masters of their own destiny. This is false. It is false in the financial services industry, and it is false in any industry. For instance, think about how your success is tied to that of your colleagues who serve as part of your team. Think about how your success is tied to your support staff. Think about how your success is tied to people who will hopefully generate referrals for you.

As we described in the section on the company C, you are considered the company even if you work for a large firm. In this case, you need to think of yourself as the company and your parent firm as a collaborator. The more successful you are at building your business, the more benefits are reaped by your parent firm. Additionally, you can position yourself as a small firm that understands the individual needs of its clients (your company) while still having the resources of a large multinational firm at your disposal (your collaborator). Lastly, you can and should develop mutually beneficial relationships with other service providers such as attorneys and accountants, who can generate an excellent referral base.

In any good marketing plan, you should do two basic things: develop a list of collaborators, and develop a plan to solve what is known as the "agency theoretic problem." That is, how do you give your collaborators incentives to operate in ways that are advantageous to you and not solely to them? This is discussed as part of the best practice tactics in Chapter 9.

THE FOUR Ps AND THEIR APPLICATION TO YOUR FINANCIAL SERVICES PRACTICE

Many marketers think of the five Cs of marketing as one's "homework," the work that has to be done to develop your strategy. Then the next step is to assimilate the information collected and determines one's *s*egmentation, *t*argeting, and *p*ositioning, or *STP* (discussed in detail in Chapter 2). Simply put, what clients will you go after (segment), by what targeted means (how), and with what basic message (positioning)? However, all of this has little to do with the "rubber meeting the road." That is, you can evaluate your five Cs, determine your STP, be mentally happy with your accomplishments, and put the result on your desk. Doing this will not affect your practice, and nothing will change. Eventually, you need to pull a tactical lever that will affect your clients and your business. The four Ps of marketing—product, promotion, place, and price—are those levers.

However, before getting into the details, we must empha-size the most basic premise of the four Ps of marketing.

Your four Ps must be aligned!

That is, the right product at the wrong price will not sell. The right product at the right price but distributed (place-ment) through the wrong channel will not sell. The right product at the right price through the right channel but with zero awareness (poor promotion) will not sell. To "sell" your financial services practice, your four Ps must be aligned. In fact, it may be bold of us to say that it would be advantageous for your practice to have the "wrong" four Ps, but aligned, rather than a misaligned set of Ps where some are right and some are wrong. There are no right Ps, ever, if they are not aligned.

Product

If you are a consumer packaged goods company selling cereal, it is fairly obvious what your product is: cereal. If you are a financial advisor in the financial services industry, what is your product? When we teach this material, we commonly start out our lectures with exactly this question: "What busi-ness are you in?" While it is a seemingly easy and innocu-ous question, it always leads to lots of discussion and debate among financial advisors, with little resolution. However, here are the most common answers we have heard:

- I help my clients holistically manage their financial goals.
- I am in the psychology business.
- My product is me.

What is most interesting is that when one merges these three answers, it is hard to argue with this definition of your product. You help individuals and families manage their financial goals. You clearly must act partly as advisor and partly as psychologist (see Chapters 5 and 6). Finally, at the end of the day, your product is you. People invest in you! We always ask how much of your client book would come with you if you were to leave your current company. One measure of a good practice for a financial advisor is a large fraction answer to this question. We would also argue that while a large fraction answer scares many large firms, they should encourage this, as successful financial advisors should be their goal as well.

Promotion

Promotion is the means by which a company informs customers about its product or service. For traditional products, these marketing vehicles include television, radio, print, direct mail, and of course the Internet, to name the major ones. While each of these vehicles is available to people working in the financial services industry, some are more prevalent and likely to be effective than others. We discuss this in detail in Chapter 8. However, for now, let us pose the following question: what would make you most aware of and likely to consider and use someone for an important purchase, like your financial advisor? The answer, suggested earlier, is referrals. Later in this book, we talk about explicit tactics to build your referral network. This is not to say that other promotional vehicles are not important. They are, but referrals are the most influential source that must be utilized as a strategic asset. In Chapter 7, when we talk about customer relationship management, we will further discuss the use of customer-level targeting that can most easily be implemented through a strong Internet targeting engine.

Placement

Placement refers to the distribution channel (e.g., a retail store) through which a customer acquires the given product or service. For the financial services industry, it is not clear that this mapping is too direct. However, let us emphasize the following: although placement (distribution) is the "most forgotten P" in many businesses, it is the most enduring one and can provide a great source of competitive advantage. Consider the following example, and then let us see the mapping to the financial services industry. Imagine a manufacturer of electronics products that strikes a deal with Best Buy to nationally and exclusively distribute its product in a given product category. Then, by definition, Best Buy's share of the market must be 100 percent. Furthermore, distribution contracts tend to be of a longer-term nature and hence enduring. Now, for someone in the financial services industry, what would be an analogous "locked-up" distribution channel? While these are likely to be less formal or less frequent, an analogous situation might be a financial advisor who has a direct referral arrangement with a particular law firm, a particular university, a given hospital, or some similar institution. In essence, the greater the degree to which you can become the preferred or, even more importantly, the *default* provider of services for a given channel, the better this will be for your practice.

Price

As with product, for many companies it is obvious what one's price means—the actual financial amount paid for the product or service. For your practice, there are your fees, but even by this early part of the book, we assume you know that we do not mean just that when we refer to price. Yes, you have fees, and we do not mean to imply that they cannot be a strategic lever. But there are at least three problems with using fees as a strategic lever. Let us start with the two easiest problems first.

First and foremost, many clients are often not directly aware of the amount of fees that they pay, and by positioning one's practice as having low fees, one is bringing greater salience to a cost. While objectively your fees may be lower, your clients' overall satisfaction with the firm may not actually be increased. In fact, much literature on customer satisfaction shows that focusing on cost minimization as opposed to customer relationships and revenues decreases satisfaction.[4]

Second, fees as a form of price have strong reference points.[5] That is, the price that you pay today is not evaluated in isolation, but rather in comparison to an internal sense of "fairness/price," which is affected strongly by your past prices and also by competitors' prices. The implication of this for your practice is both simple and multifold. If you drop your price, eventually that price (those fees) will become the reference level, and your clients will expect it and gain no extra satisfaction from that price drop. Your margin will feel it, but not your customers. Also, the impact of price changes is asymmetric. While people enjoy price cuts, they abhor price increases. So, imagine a financial advisor who changes his assets under management fee from 2 percent of assets to 1.5 percent of assets and then back to 2 percent of assets. Although this is somewhat counterintuitive, the net utility from these two price changes is likely to be negative because of what marketing/psychologists call prospect theory.[6] In Chapter 6, we will discuss the implications of prospect theory for your financial services practice more broadly, but with regard to price it is much easier to drop than to raise prices effectively, and hence once you go down a price-cutting path, it is hard to head back upstream.

The most subtle impact of price cuts has been studied widely in the economics and marketing literature through the concept of a prisoner's dilemma game.[7] Before we discuss this game and its role in the financial services industry, we emphasize that prisoner's dilemma problems are not just applicable to price, but can be related to things like discounts, service levels, giveaways, coupons, and so on. While we will be using the language and an example here of price, the theory derived by economists in game-theoretic applications is directly applicable to other parts of your practice.

To describe the prisoner's dilemma problem for the financial services industry, imagine a situation in which there are two clients, each with $10 million to invest (call them Client 1 and Client 2), one of whom is currently a client of the first firm (call it Firm A) and the other is a client of the second firm (call it Firm B). For simplicity, also assume that each firm currently charges the same assets under management fee of 2 percent but is considering lowering its fee to 1.5 percent. Consider the 2 × 2 table of decisions and payouts in Figure 1.1.

Figure 1.1 Both Firms Lose Money because of Price Cuts—Outcome and Payoff Matrix for a Prisoner's Dilemma Game

		Firm A	
		2%	1.5%
Firm B	2%	($200,000, $200,000)	($300,000, $0)
	1.5%	($0, $300,000)	($150,000, $150,000)

As we can see, if both firms stay with their 2 percent fee, they each earn 2% × $10 million = $200,000 in revenue (the status quo). However, if we look at the payouts for Firm A, then Firm A is better off cutting its fees to 1.5 percent regardless of the actions of Firm B. If Firm B does not cut its fees, Firm A gets both clients, worth a total of $20 million under management; that is, the $300,000 from the [1.5%, 2%] cell is better than the $200,000 it would receive from the [2%, 2%] cell. However, if Firm B cuts its fees, the $150,000 that Firm A would receive from the [1.5%, 1.5%] cell is more than the $0 it would receive from the [2%, 1.5%] cell. Thus, the dominant strategy for Firm A is to drop its fee rate to 1.5 percent. Clearly, since the matrix in Figure 1.1 is symmetric, this is seemingly the optimal strategy for Firm B as well, and hence both firms should rationally drop their fees to 1.5 percent. However, we note that under this scenario, both firms are *worse off*, as they both end up with 1.5% × $10 million = $150,000 where they earn $200,000 now.

Thus, the prisoner's dilemma points out the danger of using easily replicable tactics to gain a short-term advantage: the other firm can match that advantage, and both firms are then worse off. Consumers are better off, as they now have to pay only 1.5 percent fees, but both firms lose money. Note that the prisoner's dilemma problem has been recognized as one factor that has led to the lack of profitability of the airline industry,[8] as one firm offers frequent flyer miles that are then matched by a competitor firm (benefiting neither differentially). Then the first firm escalates things and offers frequent flyer miles and bonus miles for booking online, and this is quickly matched and possibly even surpassed by the competing firm. Again, as in Figure 1.1, there is no positive differential gained by either firm, and the consumer benefits at the expense of both firms.

A reasonable question is, how does one prevent prisoner's dilemmas from happening in your local market in the first place? One way, which is illegal, is explicit collusion. Both firms agree to maintain higher prices (or whatever the variable is), which works to the benefit of both firms. Without the possibility of explicit collusion, it comes down to the basic idea of signaling. For example, imagine that Firm A announces a "low price guarantee" where it states to the world that any price cut made by its competitors will be matched without question. Firm B now has no incentive to cut prices (assuming that the signal from Firm A is credible), and hence prices stay at [2%, 2%]. Thus, ironically, and not well known, lower price guarantees typically lead to higher prices, not lower prices.

A second common mechanism to try to get a market to stay at the "better" solution ([2%, 2%]) is what is known as a tit-for-tat response mechanism.[9] That is, imagine that Firm A and Firm B know that they are competing with each other for Client 1 and Client 2 over a long time horizon. A tit-for-tat strategy would say that you must "punish" defectors, and hence if you are Firm A, you must cut fees every time Firm B does, and vice versa. This signals clearly to the opposing firm that any defections from the superior outcome for both firms jointly will be dealt with immediately, again signaling the intent of the firm. While this simplified example in Figure 1.1 highlights just one small fraction of the prisoner's dilemma problem, it indicates the types of strategic decisions that you must make.

Returning to price more broadly, the reason why we mention that fees are just one part of price is the important role that transaction costs play as a determinant of the "price" of doing business. Imagine that Firm A drops its fees to 1.5 percent but simultaneously raises the amount of time it takes to get called back. Clients 1 and 2 are now trading off fees against service time, for which there is no obvious answer. Thus, when you and your practice are thinking about price, think about the price-to-value ratio that you are providing and try to deliver greater value at a given price level.

WHY A CLIENT-CENTRIC ORIENTATION ALWAYS PAYS

Let us get straight to the heart of the matter now. Will a client-centric orientation lower your costs in the short run? Unlikely. A client-centric orientation is likely to cost you what is possibly your greatest asset, time. Since it takes time to be customer-centric, when acquisition and retention costs are incorporated, in fact it may cost you when you measure yourself on common measures of success (number of clients) in the *short run*. Will a client-centric orientation generate increased revenue immediately? It's unclear. A client-centric orientation is about building relationships, which will help you acquire the type of clients that you want and retain them for the long run. That is, in Chapter 7 we will provide a detailed discussion of how a client-centric orientation may raise acquisition costs but also significantly raise the value of the customers acquired and the likelihood of retention. It is this short-term-versus-long-term trade-off that lies at the center of a quantitative look at a client-centric versus a revenue-centric firm. Lastly, it is important to mention that a client-centric orientation does not preclude or reduce the importance of profit maximization, as some may believe; rather, just the opposite. A better way to think about it is that a client-centric orientation recognizes that profitability happens one customer at a time, and a client-centric view of your asset book will focus on the heterogeneity among customers and develop ways to maximize it (including the firing of some of those customers).

LOOKING FORWARD

This chapter has tried to introduce you to some of the jargon and structure of marketing as applied to the financial services industry, as well as to the five Cs (customer, company, competition, context, and collaborators) and four Ps (product, promotion, place, and price) framework for thinking about your practice. However, we have not lost sight of the fact that our ultimate goal is to help you construct a marketing plan to improve your practice. The remaining chapters cover the following aspects of that plan, with the following brief preview.

Chapters 2 and 3: Segmentation and Niche Strategies.
Segmentation is the process by which groups of homo-
geneous clients with similar needs and characteristics are
identified. We discuss in Chapter 2 how to use client-
level data that are commonly available to financial advisors to form segments of customers. Unlike the ways in
which clients are commonly segmented, such as assets
under management, we demonstrate an improved set of
approaches that allows for superior targeting and product differentiation. Once those segments are formed,
you must select the target segment(s) [niche market(s)]
on which you are going to focus. Chapter 3 contains
both some thoughts on selecting target markets that
make the most sense for your financial practice and a
description of our survey results that describe a number
of niches that our respondents commonly use.

Chapter 4: Branding. In this chapter, we discuss the
fundamental role that branding plays in your practice.
Branding is that aspect of your practice that uniquely
differentiates it from competitors' practices and allows
you to represent your core value proposition. Your
brand is your most valuable asset, and we will map out
ways to build and enhance it.

***Chapters 5 and 6: Decision Making and Investor
Psychology.*** While everyone wants to believe that the
drivers of choice for his product or service are mostly
unique, data suggest otherwise. In particular, we present here the basic steps of decision choice, including
awareness, consideration set formation, preference formation, and ultimate choice, explaining along the way
the impact that you can have on each stage. In addition,

we recognize that investing is a large-stakes, uncertain series of decisions and that clients do not always act in their own best interest. We will discuss a wide range of psychological research and theory to help you better understand and serve your clients.

Chapter 7: Client Relationship Management. A method central to marketing that allows you to identify profitable clients is the computation of client lifetime value (CLV). This technique is described through hypothetical examples. Furthermore, its application to maximizing financial advisor practice performance is described in detail.

Chapter 8: Advertising and Promotion. As we have described in this chapter, and as will be described in Chapters 5 and 6, it is important to be able to influence clients at various stages of their decision processes. We will describe advertising and promoting yourself and your practice effectively and in a credible way that is entirely consistent with your brand. Our focus will be on describing which forms of advertising are most effective in the financial services industry, depending on the purpose, and suggesting ways to increase the effectiveness of advertising.

Chapter 9: Tactics. While Chapters 1 through 8 discuss both theory and the results of our survey of financial advisors, Chapter 9 presents tactics that you can use to improve your practice in the short term. These tactics include developing your "three words" for branding, constructing your advisory board, and forming your word-of-mouth army, to name a few. This chapter highlights the best practices of the most effective FAs in our surveys.

Chapter 10: Marketing Plan. Obviously, we hope that Chapters 1 through 9 provide you with the details that you need to construct your one-page marketing plan. However, the best way to cement the ideas presented throughout this book is to provide you with a hypothetical sample plan that you can emulate immediately. Chapter 10 provides this and includes advice for starting your transformation to a client-centric practice.

In summary, we return to our goals for the readers of this book. We want you to leave this book with a marketing plan that is concise, provides you with a clear statement of the differential value that you have for a target segment of clients, and allows you to improve your profitability by acquiring and retaining the right customers. This is simply said; now the work begins!

NOTES

1. For reasons of confidentiality, we will refer to the firms we have worked with generically. All programs have been run through the Aresty Executive Education Institute at the Wharton School of the University of Pennsylvania.

2. Capgemini and Merrill Lynch, "World Wealth Report 2008"; http://www.ml.com/media/100472.pdf.

3. Kevin Lane Keller and Philip Kotler, *Marketing Management*, 13th ed. (Upper Saddle River, N.J.: Prentice Hall, 2009).

4. Eugene W. Anderson, Claes Fornell, and Roland T. Rust, "Customer Satisfaction, Productivity, and Profitability: Differences between Goods and Services," *Marketing Science* 16, no. 2 (1997), 129–148; Ruth N. Bolton and Katherine N. Lemon, "A Dynamic Model of Customers' Usage of Services: Usage as an Antecedent and Consequence of Satisfaction," *Journal of Marketing Research* 36, no. 2 (May 1999), 171–186.

5. Bruce G. S. Hardie, Eric J. Johnson, and Peter S. Fader, "Modeling Loss Aversion and Reference Dependence Effects on Brand Choice," *Marketing Science* 12, no. 4 (1993), 378–395; Russel S. Winer, "A Multi-Stage Model of Choice Incorporating Reference Prices," *Marketing Letters* 1, no. 1 (December 1989), 27–36.

6. Daniel Kahneman and Amos Tversky, "Prospect Theory: An Analysis of Decision under Risk," *Econometrica* 47 (1979), 263–291.

7. John Nash, "Equilibrium Points in n-Person Games," *Proceedings of the National Academy of Sciences* 36, no. 1 (1950), 48–49.

8. Kim Byung-Do, Shi Mengze, and Kannan Srinivasan, "Reward Programs and Tacit Collusion," *Marketing Science* 20, no. 2 (2001), 99–121

9. Robert Aumann, "Acceptable Points in General Cooperative n-Person Games," *Contributions to the Theory of Games IV*, Annals of Mathematics Study 40 (Princeton, N.J.: Princeton University Press, 1959), pp. 287–324; Robert Axelrod, "Effective Choice in the Prisoner's Dilemma," *Journal of Conflict Resolution* 24, no. 1 (March 1980), 3–25.

CHAPTER 2

SEGMENTATION

If you were to write down the terms and concepts that would be in the marketing "Hall of Fame," the five Cs (customers, company, competition, context, and collaborators) and the four Ps (product, price, place, and promotion) would be the lead-off hitters. Doing your five Cs and four Ps first makes sense. In other words, how can you know what to do if you don't know where you are?

However, the next batter, if not the clean-up hitter, would have to be STP: *s*egmentation, *t*argeting and *p*ositioning. STP, ironically what many call the "oil" that makes the marketing engine go, refers to the process whereby a financial services firm would

- List potential and current clients.
- Break that list into segments or groups of clients: segmentation.
- Evaluate those segments to determine their overall attractiveness.

- Select from among those segments the clients to focus on: targeting.
- Determine the marketing mix—product, price, place, and promotion—that you would use for each of those segments: positioning.

Segmentation is recognizing that different clients want different things and that not all clients share the same underlying preferences for the products and services that a financial advisor (FA) might offer. Because different customer segments want different things, they will also feel better served, and more satisfied, if you can give them exactly what they want and nothing else. Given a broad assortment of preferences for different types of services and products, an FA will want to carefully choose which segments she wishes to focus on.

Note two key aspects of STP. First and foremost, segmentation involves *sacrifice*—i.e., the realization that no successful financial advisor can be everything to everyone. You cannot serve all potential clients. There are some that you will decide to walk away from. In fact, to be successful, you have to select only the types of clients that you can serve most effectively. And your choice of customer segments to focus on should be based on data.

Some may say, "What? I have to ignore a set of potential clients that are not in the chosen set?" This is not exactly what we are saying. The key to a successful practice, and to a successful brand, as will be discussed in Chapter 4, is an unambiguous, clear, and memorable positioning. Through segmentation, you select the *best* customers and position yourself differentially and effectively toward exactly those customers.

"But why can't I have them all?" many people ask. Well, consider a positioning in which a financial advisor decides to be "service-oriented." First, to be service-oriented to all clients might be too time-consuming. Instead, you should focus on those segments that will be most sensitive to increases in service levels. Second, for some client groups, service is not the primary driver of their financial advisor choice, investment, and retention. Instead, costs, the portfolio of services available, or other factors may be most important for that client group. Further, what constitutes excellent service might vary by segment. Using one positioning would not appropriately address these groups' differential needs.

The second key aspect of segmentation is cost, or, "What do you mean I need a different set of four Ps for each segment?" Yes, you do. That is the reason you should segment the market. By providing different sets of services, positioned differently, you are able to provide greater value to each segment. You can provide exactly what a particular segment wants across the entire set of Ps. Now you should ask, "What do I get for this cost?" Well, if you believe in segmentation, then what you will receive is pretty impressive:

- Lower acquisition costs, as your positioning will be more in line with the target client you are trying to attract
- Greater retention, as clients are more likely to stay with a financial advisor who provides them with products and services that are more tailored to their needs
- A larger dollar wallet share of clients' assets under management, as advisors who provide superior products and service are more trusted

- Finally, economies of scale, as advisors who focus on segments build enough critical mass in a segment to "cross the chasm"[1] and become synonymous with and in the consideration set of clients

Next, we describe in more detail the value of segmentation, the data needed to do it, and what you should do with your segments once you have them.

WHAT IS SEGMENTATION?

To illustrate segmentation and the benefits it provides to your practice, consider Figure 2.1.

On one end of the spectrum, we see one-to-one marketing, implying individualized service and distinctive four Ps for each and every one of your clients. That is, each client gets a unique set of products, prices, promotion strategies, and so on. While this seems appealing on the surface, it is inefficient. For instance, who would argue that clients couldn't be categorized into those who care about fees and

Figure 2.1 There Is a Middle Ground! A Schematic Representing Segmentation and Its Relationship to One-to-One Marketing and Mass Advertising

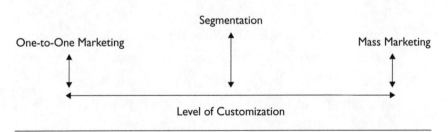

those who do not (relatively, of course)? Who would argue that there are clients who want heavy personalized service and those who do not? While it's clear that clients do want different things, this doesn't mean that you have to deliver your services in a one-to-one, completely individualized way. In fact, we say in a somewhat inflammatory way that it is hard to find a business-to-consumer situation in which true one-to-one marketing has been profitable[2]; however, this is an open debate.

On the other end of the spectrum, we see mass marketing, which may not be literal but can be interpreted as applying the same four Ps to all your clients. One set of products is sold to everyone, one price is charged to everyone, and so on. While it is hard to argue that each of one's clients is unique, it is much harder to argue that all your clients are similar enough to treat them exactly the same. However, before we start lauding segmentation as a compromise solution, it is important to note that actions speak infinitely louder than just words. If you segment your clients on paper but never implement a differential marketing mix for those clients, you will realize no value from your effort to identify segments. If you segment customers and there is no difference between what the different segments really want from you, then your segmentation scheme is valueless. Thus, segmentation is meant to be action-oriented, and its value to your financial practice will depend on your ability to deliver on the data-based segmentation scheme that you form.

Segmentation, as shown in Figure 2.1, lies directly in the middle between one-to-one and mass marketing. Rather than assuming that everyone is the same or that everyone is different, segmentation assumes that there are a discrete number of different types of clients, denoted *k*, for which the marketer will implement a different marketing mix. For instance, consider Figure 2.2, where there are *k* = 3 segments of clients who care differentially about two primary dimensions: service and fees (we will discuss later how to determine *k* and what variables to use to segment the clients). Even within a segment, there might be some range of preferences, so in Figure 2.2, the center dots represent the average client within a segment, and the arrows and corresponding clouds around the dots reflect the variety within a segment.

Segment 1 is made up of those clients who care significantly about both the service that they receive and the fees that they pay. It is important to note that this segment of

Figure 2.2 Clients Are Not All the Same: A Schematic Representing *k* = 3 Client Segments with Centers (Dots) and Arrows Representing Variation around the Center. The Vertical Axis Denotes the Importance of Service and the Horizontal Axis the Importance of Fees to a Given Client.

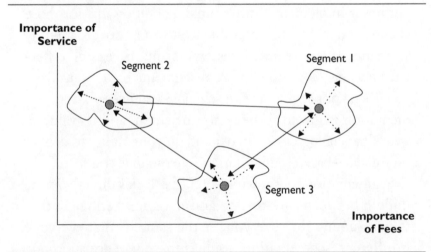

clients may, in fact, be unprofitable for this financial advisor, as the combination of both high service levels and a low "price" is difficult to provide. Segment 2 wants high service, but is less concerned about fees. This segment may indeed be attractive to the financial advisor (but also to his competitors!) if he actually can and desires to provide high service levels. As we will talk about in the next chapter, it is crucial that your segmentation strategy matches your core capabilities with the target segment. A business should target only consumers whose preferences are consistent with that business's core strengths. Finally, Segment 3 puts low importance on service and is moderately sensitive to the fees. This segment may be quite profitable to serve. We note that Segment 3 may be quite consistent with clients who are not deeply engaged with their financial advisors and do not monitor their accounts that actively. Hence, they are mostly unaware of their fees, require little service, and can be used as "cash cows," if you will, to fund other client types. The financial advisor looking at this analysis might decide that Segment 2 is the one that she prefers to target. In doing so, the FA may also decide not to pursue Segment 1, which requires much higher levels of service.

MYTH BUSTING: ONE SEGMENT IS NOT ENOUGH

One of the arguments against segmentation that is commonly made is that it restricts an advisor to a small fraction of potential clients. We respectfully disagree. For example, imagine that in your local area, you decide to focus on high-net-worth lawyers, who represent 3 percent of your potential client base. Doesn't focusing on this niche market restrict your business potential? We argue just the opposite. In fact, there is significant marketing research[3] indicating that STP is exactly the right long-run strategy and that your ability to acquire significant numbers of customers happens segment by segment. That is, you are more likely to succeed in attracting and retaining clients if you focus on giving one segment exactly what it wants. In contrast, the FA who tries to be all things to all potential clients may not be giving any individual client what she wants and ultimately becomes less attractive to everyone.

Thus, the implications for your acquisition and retention strategy become quite straightforward. Segmentation does not mean putting all your eggs in one basket and focusing only on a given segment, but rather developing a prioritized, ordered list of segments to go after and trying to attract and serve those segments one at a time. Once you obtain traction in a given segment, those effects will snowball and become multiplicative (business begets business, word of mouth generates word of mouth). In Chapter 3 we will discuss common segmentation and niche strategies used by other successful financial advisors.

One last comment is related to branding, which we discuss further in Chapter 4. When you select a segment priority list, this does not mean finding the best segment and the next best segment in isolation. Rather, it is crucial that you retain your brand consistency and select segments that will have synergistic value with each other. As an example, imagine that your primary target segment consists of physicians in your local area, and that you are considering adding attorneys as a secondary and important target segment. You might ask yourself the questions: "Do physicians and attorneys share the same decision-making processes, so that what I know about physicians can be applied to attorneys? Are physicians likely to know attorneys, so that I can get advantageous word-of-mouth referrals? Will working with attorneys damage or enhance my brand equity with physicians?" Just to reinforce this, no firm would select a set of customers to sell its product to that would alienate its core customer base; think of sequential segmentation in the same way.

SELECTING A BASIS FOR SEGMENTATION

How do you arrive at a segmentation scheme? To make this key decision, simply look at Figure 2.3, which describes the necessary data.

Imagine that Figure 2.3 is a Microsoft Excel spreadsheet of data with the rows representing clients, one row per client. Now, if we want to sort and cluster the clients according to some criteria, what variables should we put into the columns? While there are a number of possibilities, both industry practice and marketing thought suggest that firms tend to cluster clients on three basic sets of variables: demographics, behaviors, or psychographics. We discuss each of these three in turn.

Demographic segmentation would entail segmenting your clients based on variables such as age, race, gender, urban/ rural, number of children, income, and so on. These are classic variables that are collected as part of any initial application

Figure 2.3 Segmentation Is All about the Data: A Tabular Representation of Clustering, Where Each Client's Data Are Contained in a Row of the Database and the Final Outcome Is an Assignment of Each Person to One of _k_ Clusters, as Indicated on the Right

	Demographics	Age	Race			
Client 1						
Client 2						

Variables → (top header); Segment Assignment → (right column); Clients (left label)

process. There are both pluses and minuses to demographic segmentation. In terms of the pluses, it is easy to do, it is very easy to explain, the data are easy to collect, and it is usually accurately measured. On the downside, do you really believe that someone's demographic characteristics are really tied that closely to his decision-making behavior for financial services? Are all older people (for example) likely to have the same wants and needs and risk profile? Are they all likely to make decisions in the same manner? Typically, the answer to these questions is at best "maybe," and hence that is really the trade-off for this segmentation basis.

Behavioral segmentation entails segmenting clients on the basis of their behaviors in the past. For financial services advisors, these behaviors might include the amount of assets under management (perhaps categorized as low, medium, and high), the types of products or services they have previously purchased from your firm or from a competitor (e.g., retirement, insurance, or estate plans), and length of tenure with the firm. As with all segmentation bases, there are considerable pluses and minuses. On the plus side, what predicts future behavior better than past behavior? Furthermore, this is recognized in some sense as the de facto standard: we treat big clients differently from smaller ones; we treat retirement-focused clients differently from wealth-acquisition-oriented ones; we treat longtime clients differently from new arrivals. There is a lot to say for this line of reasoning. On the negative side, the logic of using past behavior is somewhat flawed. For instance, imagine that you have acquired clients in the past and obtained assets under management under a given segmentation scheme (or lack thereof), a given targeting, and a given positioning strategy. Now you change that strategy as a result of a formal assessment of your segments. One could easily imagine that the past data will be far from indicative of the future, and therefore using past behavior and then changing policy will not lead to good future targeting of clients.

Lastly, we talk about a segmentation basis that is likely to be most unfamiliar to our readers: psychographic segmentation. Psychographic segmentation uses variables from individual clients, typically collected via surveys, concerning those individuals' psychological characteristics. Variables in this set typically include questions about activities, interests, opinions, attitudes, and values. The concept behind psychographic segmentation is quite logical: people use products and services that satisfy some fundamental psychological need. For instance, "safety-oriented" individuals tend to shy away from risky products and services and buy products and services that give them a sense of comfort. This is true regardless of the product category, whether it is child seats or conservative stock picks or the type of life insurance they select. It is hard to imagine that you would not want to have this information, as it would affect how you talk to these individuals, how you select products and services to recommend to them, and so on.

At the other extreme, "outdoorsy" people tend to be more adventurous and to buy products and services that meet those needs. These people have a wholly different mindset (are in a different segment) from safety-oriented clients, and the FA's entire four Ps (product, price, promotion, and placement) strategy directed toward them could be entirely different. Now, just as with the other segmentation bases mentioned, psychographics has its theoretical and conceptual upside, yet it also has a very practical set of downsides. These are described in detail in a later section, but they include the ability to measure someone's psychological profile easily and the ability to act on it in a meaningful way.

Segmentation variables are certainly not limited to the three categories just described. When we discuss segmentation with advisors, the single most common variable used to categorize clients is amount of investable assets. While this is certainly of interest to all FAs and would probably be included in any segmentation of financial services customers, it is not sufficient by itself to really create a meaningful, marketing-based distinction. Another important variable that many successful advisors consider is benefits sought. That is, why are people investing in the first place? It could be that two clients with the same demographic and psychographic profile are investing for two completely different reasons. One client may be looking to build wealth for an early retirement, while another is simply looking to protect assets and minimize risk. The message is that the variables you choose should be tied to some meaningful outcome that is actionable.

HOW MANY SEGMENTS OF CLIENTS?

We next discuss another issue related to segmentation: selecting the *number* of segments. Let us first explain why this is not a simple problem or one where you can just "let the computer do it for you." One common criterion used to determine the number of segments involves maximizing between-cluster variability and minimizing within-cluster variability. Stated another way, you want the individuals within a segment to be as like one another as possible, called low within-cluster variability. But you want the individuals in different segments to be as unlike one another as possible. Referring back to Figure 2.2, you want to make the center dots as far apart from each other as possible (maximizing between-cluster variability) and make the arrows within segments as small as possible (minimizing within-cluster variability). In fact, a way in which most people operationalize this is via what is called an "elbow" or "scree" plot.[4] In a scree plot, you plot the residual sum of squares (RSS), equal to the sum of within-segment variation added across clusters (this is obtainable directly from computer output), on the y-axis against the number of clusters on the x-axis. An example of a scree plot is given in Figure 2.4, which indicates that $k = 3$ segments is reasonable.

Figure 2.4 How Many Segments? Look For the "Elbow"! A Scree Plot Shows the Total Error of a Segmentation Scheme Plotted against the Number of Segments. The Bend, or Elbow, in This Scree Plot Happens at $k = 3$ Segments, Indicating that Adding More Segments Does Not Improve the Segmentation Scheme Dramatically

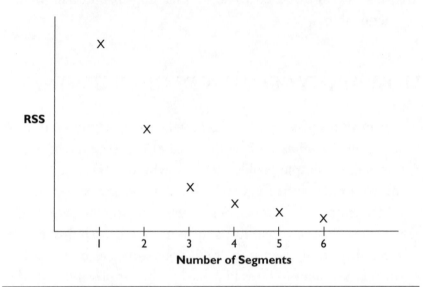

The problem with this criterion is it sometimes leads to too many may segments being suggested. It almost appears as if each client might as well be in its own segment. However, there are business costs associated with having too many segments, such as increased internal corporate costs resulting from having more brands to manage for different clients, lost economies of scale, and increased client confusion.[5] Therefore, we discuss other criteria for determining the value of a segmentation scheme in the next section.

HOW DO YOU KNOW IF YOU HAVE A GOOD SEGMENTATION SCHEME FOR YOUR FINANCIAL SERVICES CLIENTS?

While marketers rarely all agree on everything or even anything, there is universal agreement that for a segmentation scheme to be useful in practice, it should score highly on the following five critical dimensions.[6] Thus, when considering bases for segmentation, one should evaluate those segmentation schemes on the following criteria.

Relevant: Do Segments Actually Respond Differently?

It is hard to argue against relevance as a segmentation criterion. Imagine that you are segmenting your clients into three classes on the basis of their assets under management: ultra-high-net-worth (above $10 million), medium-to-large (between $1 and $10 million), and small-to-medium (under $1 million) clients. This segmentation is utterly worthless if these segments do not behave differently on some action-oriented variable that you care about. For instance, imagine that the impact of fees, acquisition strategy, wants and needs, and other variables are identical across segments. Then the segmentation strategy is not relevant. Alternatively, it might be that the segments of clients behave markedly differently, but on things that are not of value to your financial practice.

Measurable: Can You Describe and Quantify Segment Membership in General?

If you cannot measure the variable that you use to segment clients, then you cannot assign clients to segments; hence, your segmentation scheme is not valuable. For example, some argue that this is the case with many psychographic segmentation variables. How can you really measure someone's risk profile? How can you really measure someone's safety orientation? How can you really measure someone's values and desires? While you can give your clients a battery of survey items, the clients must be willing to answer the questions, and there are often errors in the measurements. In contrast, demographic and behavioral segments are easily measured. We believe that by using careful methods, you can measure psychographic variables. Moreover, these variables are often more meaningful than the more easily measured demographic or behavioral variables.

Sizable: Is the Potential Segment Big Enough to Warrant Special Attention?

Suppose you determine that there are three segments of your clients, the first with 60 percent of your potential clients, the second with 39 percent, and the last with 1 percent. Would you really develop a separate four Ps strategy for just 1 percent of your potential clients? You might if that 1 percent generated 15 percent of your income and revenues, but in general, segments need to be large enough, either in number or in scale, to justify their existence and your offer to serve them.

Identifiable, Reachable, and Accessible: Can You Identify and Address Segment Members in a Targeted Way?

One of the common sets of questions that is included in most studies relates to media habits, such as television viewing, magazine reading, Internet sites visited, and so on. The purpose of this is so that after clients have been assigned to segments (as in Figure 2.2), you can reach these segments in order to communicate your relevance to them. Without this, you can state that there is a big segment out there, it is measurable, and it is characterized by a feature that you care about, but unfortunately there is no way to get your message to these people. We note, however, that not being able to get your message to your clients is probably a matter of degree. Usually you can reach these clients, but can you do it in a simple and efficient way? This criterion also suggests that you need a distribution channel to sell to your clients. Imagine, for example, that you want to try to attract clients from a particular segment, but a competitor already has a strong dominating presence. Clearly, this should lower the value of this segment, as it is likely to be less accessible.

Compatible with Resources: Is the Segmentation Scheme Useful for You, Given Your Resources?

There are no right or wrong segments, but there are right or wrong segments for *you*. Segments that are inconsistent with your resources (for example, the conversion rate is too low), your personality (for example, your persona does not mesh well with the segment), or your brand should not be considered. We next discuss how to construct a segmentation scheme operationally.

HOW TO OBTAIN MARKET SEGMENTS OF CLIENTS

As this book is meant to be action-oriented, we provide a set of step-by-step directions for segmenting your clients in Figure 2.5.

Figure 2.5 Client Segmentation Methodology from Start to Finish

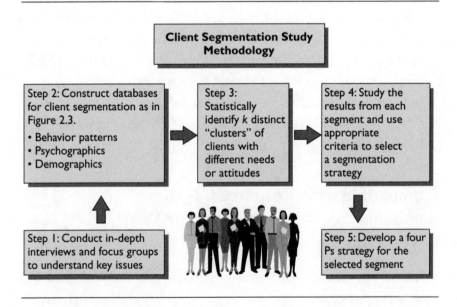

Step 1: Conduct Exploratory Research

Before embarking on any study of clients, it is important to understand the basic issues. For instance, what are the drivers of client choice? What are the drivers of retention for clients? What are clients' general areas of satisfaction and dissatisfaction with their current FA? There are many sources of exploratory information to provide these answers; however, three ways tend to be most popular: your insight, one-on-one client interviews, and focus groups.

While using your insight might not seem like the most scientific way possible, it is extremely valuable. If you are looking to understand the segments within your own practice that may be reflective of segments in the wider population, this can be a great place to start. Who knows your clients better than you do? To bring more formalism to this process, we suggest that you do two things. First and foremost, collect informal feedback from all your clients each and every time you meet or talk with them. This should be done in a spreadsheet format so that you can code the responses later. Second, perform a SWOT (strengths, weaknesses, opportunities, and threats)[7] analysis every year to update the progress that you have made in your practice.

Each and every year, construct a 2 × 2 spreadsheet of your strengths and weaknesses as you perceive them, opportunities for expanding your business, and finally threats to you and your financial services practice (see Figure 2.6). While it is never clear that much action is taken based on SWOT analysis, we prefer to view it a different way. Forcing yourself to think about these things, when most financial advisors normally do not, will aid you in thinking strategically about your business, and that is always a good thing.

One-on-one interviews with your existing clients are what you routinely do anyway when you have annual or semiannual meetings. Thus, this "data collection" method for feedback is marginally costless; yet, more importantly, how many financial service advisors have a sufficient relationship with their

Figure 2.6 SWOT Analysis Matrix

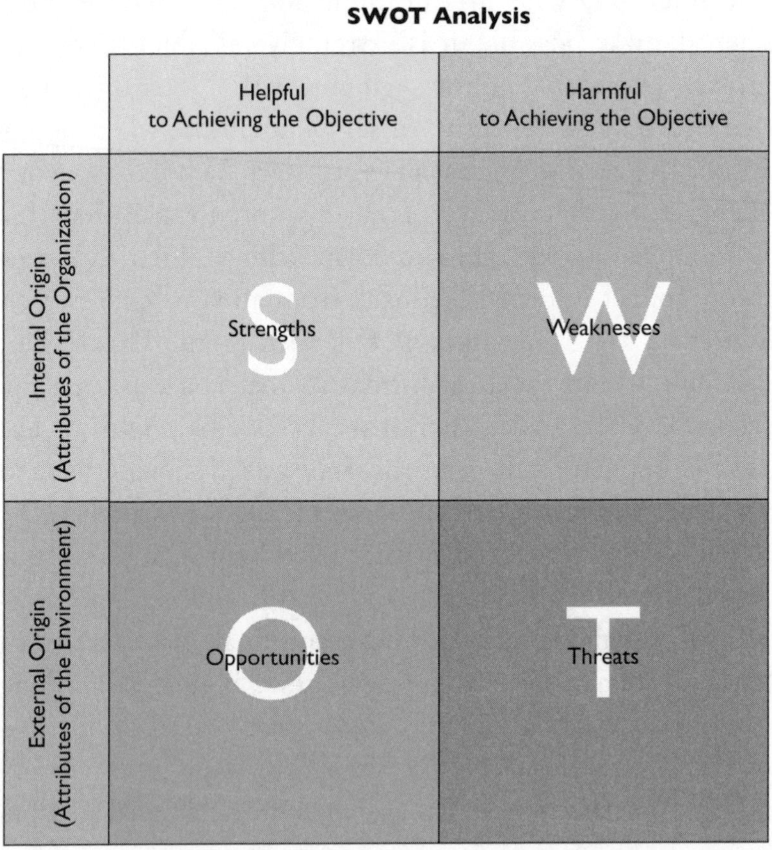

SWOT Analysis

	Helpful to Achieving the Objective	Harmful to Achieving the Objective
Internal Origin (Attributes of the Organization)	**S** Strengths	**W** Weaknesses
External Origin (Attributes of the Environment)	**O** Opportunities	**T** Threats

clients that they can speak with them in an open way, not only about the clients' financial needs, but also about the FA's service of those needs? Thus, it is important to develop a specific group of clients that can give you such feedback—what we call a "board of advisors" that can help steer your practice. Chapter 9 will give you further details on this tactic. While your knowledge is valuable, as we discuss throughout the book, it is clients' perceptions of you that matter most. Hence, even if you think you know your clients well, it is important to augment your knowledge with client perceptions.

Last, we discuss a more formal procedure for collecting consumer insights that can be quite valuable: focus groups,[8] which are the "800-pound gorilla" as a method of exploratory consumer data collection. Although there are many models for how focus groups work, typically they run as follows. Through a professional organization, you obtain a professional moderator and a "neutral" off-site location that is not affiliated with your business. This is key, and it will be discussed later. Eight to ten clients in your target segment are invited to spend 1 to 1.5 hours discussing their needs and goals with respect to financial services. If you are focused on understanding the status of your current practice better, you might also ask that they spend time discussing you and your practice. Furthermore, this off-site location typically has videotaping equipment or a one-way mirror so that you can actually observe the responses of the clients and not just read a transcript afterwards of what went on. Hearing directly from clients is one of the most powerful parts of the experience. In our opinion, videotaping is preferable, as you can then go back and take a more objective view of the focus group after the "initial buzz or shock" has worn off.

The focus group moderator then spends the time probing clients about their financial needs and desires and perhaps also about ways in which you are excelling, ways in which you can improve, and general insights about how your brand is perceived among your existing clients. Of course, most clients will not attend lengthy focus group sessions for free, and thus they need to be provided with incentives. Focus group fees can range from a low of $10 if your target segment of interest is students to as much as $400 to $500 per participant if you are "buying" physicians' or lawyers' time. In total, a typical focus group may cost between $5,000 and $7,500, between the incentive fees and the payment for the moderator and firm. Note, however, that online focus groups are now becoming more common and can reduce costs substantially; i.e., by as much as 75 percent over standard focus groups.

As noted earlier, you may be tempted to do it yourself. Why not just get someone to invite clients and moderate the session? You can save money and possibly even run it at your own location in your own conference room. This can be a mistake for a number of reasons. First, focus groups are designed to generate honest client feedback, and holding them in your office will reduce the likelihood of getting this. Second, the moderator must be seen as neutral and must not be seen as fishing for one type of answer or another. Finally, a focus group may sound like a free-flowing, freewheeling, wide-open unstructured discussion. But if it is done appropriately, it is far from that. In fact, a good professional firm will interview both you and a few clients in a one-on-one fashion to understand the basic key issues first so that the moderator has a script of ideas to utilize for a subsequent focus group session. In our collective experience, which includes running, observing, and utilizing focus groups, we find them incredibly valuable and eye-opening. In fact, we have observed many clients who are in a state of shock (both positive and negative) as a result of what they hear.

In the financial services industry, it can seem strange to ask clients to participate in a focus group. That is, it is not the norm to ask people who may be investing $100,000 to $10 million or more with you to sit and give you feedback in a group setting. We agree, and that is why we suggest two things. First, when you select eight to ten clients to attend the focus group, make sure that they are from the *same* target segment. Heterogeneity in people's interests and backgrounds is nice as a totality for your insights, but not within a single focus group session.

And choose carefully when you send out those original invitations. Recently, an FA told us that she had held a focus group and that it had gone terribly awry. She invited a high-profile local businessman for whom she currently managed about 20 percent of his portfolio. He worked with another advisor on the rest of his portfolio, and this FA was looking to understand how she could gain more of his business. However, she also invited five or six other clients for whom she was the only advisor. As soon as the discussion began, the first client started explaining his philosophy about the value of having multiple advisors. Immediately, the other clients in the room felt that they too should consider working with more than one advisor, and the FA's exclusive relationship with each of them was jeopardized.

Second, don't ask your clients to "attend a focus group," as that sounds way too impersonal. Instead, ask them to "partner with you" to improve your practice. Everyone wants to be a partner and to seem like part of the team. When we discuss the establishment of a board of advisors for your practice in Chapter 9, we will describe additional ways to research your clients.

Step 2: Construct Your Segmentation Database

As we described in Figure 2.3, the first operational step in segmenting the market is to construct a database in which each of the rows corresponds to a particular client and each column corresponds to a different variable that you will utilize for segmenting the market. For instance, if you are doing demographic segmentation, these might be age, race, number of children, and education. If you have chosen a behavioral basis for segmentation, then each column might record a different aspect of the clients' behavior, such as amount of assets under management, length of relationship with their current FA (or you), number of different financial products that they utilize, and so on. Finally, as described earlier, if you are interested in segmenting people based on psychographics, then each column of this database would contain that individual client's "score" on one of the psychographic questions. This matrix of clients by variables is what a computer program that will do the segmentation requires as a set of inputs. Most computer programs will not have a "market segmentation button," but rather a set of buttons or routines that are labeled as "cluster analysis," the statistical technique that is most commonly used to form market segments.

Step 3: Identify k Distinct Clusters

Once the matrix of information is input into a cluster analysis routine, you have to select the type of clustering algorithm you want to use. While there are many, the most common one is called "k-means clustering," where k refers to the number of clusters to be formed and *means* refers to the fact that each cluster will be described by its cluster mean (see Figure 2.2, as that pictorially describes k-means clustering). Other cluster algorithms include fuzzy clustering (where clients are probabilistically assigned to clusters, e.g., there is a 70 percent chance that a client is in one cluster and a 30 percent chance that he is in another) and hierarchical clustering (two clients are joined into a cluster, then the next nearest client is joined to them, and so on).

The process then follows what is suggested in Figure 2.4, where you run the k-means clustering algorithm for $k = 2$, 3, or more clusters, plot the error sums of squares (part of the standard output), and look at the segment sizes to determine the optimal number of clusters. Again, when the error sums of squares stop dropping rapidly and/or the new clusters being formed are minuscule in size and thus are of little business relevance, then it is time to stop adding clusters and the value of the optimal k is the number of clusters of clients that you will utilize.

Step 4: Determine the Appropriate Basis for Segmentation

Imagine that you have demographic, behavioral, and psychographic (survey) data on your clients. Then you can form market segments using each of the three separately, but which is best? This is exactly where the aforementioned criteria for an effective segmentation scheme come in.

You should construct a segmentation scorecard (see Figure 2.7), evaluate each of the three potential segmentations that come out along the five criteria, and choose the one that has the best segmentation properties. You could simply rate each segmentation scheme according to some score. For example, you might allocate 10 points to each of the five dimensions. So, you would rate the relevance of the demographic segmentation scheme from 0 to 10, then the measurability of the demographic segmentation scheme from 0 to 10, and so on. Each segmentation scheme thus might be assigned an aggregate overall score ranging from 0 (scoring 0 on each dimension) to 50 (scoring 10 on each dimension). Alternatively, you might decide to assign importance weights to each dimension. You might do this if you think that relevance and size are more important than any of the other dimensions and thus should account for more of the overall score for any segmentation scheme. You might weight the dimensions by a factor between 0 and 1, perhaps. For instance, if relevant, measurable, and sizable have weights of 0.9, identifiable a weight of 0.7, and compatible a weight of 0.5, and you score a given segmentation scheme as (9, 8, 8, 9, 5) on these dimensions, then the weighted score $= 0.9 \times 9 + 0.9 \times 8 + 0.9 \times 8 + 0.7 \times 9 + 0.5 \times 5 = 31.3$, and this score could then be compared to the weighted score for the other two potential segmentations.

Figure 2.7 Which Segmentation Scheme Should You Select?
A Segmentation Scorecard

	Relevant	Measurable	Sizable	Identifiable	Compatible
Demographic					
Behavioral					
Psychographic					

Step 5: Develop a Four Ps Strategy for a Given Segment

Once you have identified k segments, it is time to do the rest of STP (segmentation, targeting, and positioning): decide which segment(s) to focus your efforts on (T = targeting) and then develop the marketing mix (P = positioning) for those segments. Clearly, when you are selecting which segments to target, this is where the behavioral data that you have collected (regardless of whether that is the basis you have used to segment your clients or not) become relevant. The most common variables used to determine the attractiveness of a given potential client segment are assets under management (segment size), growth potential of the segment, compatibility between you and the segment, and strategic value of the segment. While there is no guarantee that there will be a clear winner, there usually is. There is typically one identified segment of clients that is in your "sweet spot."

Lastly, once you have selected that segment, you can determine the proper price, product, placement, and promotion to deliver to it. Regarding price, it may not literally be the price (fees) you are charging the clients (although it could be), but rather the cost to them of doing business with you. What are the significant financial and time drivers of the segment, and how can you match the clients' needs? For product, this is where segmentation really plays a significantly advantageous role. This is where you develop a prototypical profile of a client for this segment and determine how she makes choices, what drives her, what benefits she is seeking, and what her goals are. These are topics we discuss throughout the remainder of the book. The "place" decision for a given segment is your method of reaching the people in the segment with your offerings. As financial advisors, you don't really physically distribute your product; instead, you provide information via e-mail, phone, Internet, and so on. Which is the preferred method for this segment? Finally, with regard to promotion, it is all is about how to get your message out. Is advertising appropriate? And if so, in what publications, and what should the message be? Is word of mouth appropriate, and can you do it efficiently? Thus, understanding how this particular segment makes decisions will allow you to understand the best promotional avenues to reach it.

SUMMARY AND OVERVIEW OF SEGMENTATION

This chapter has laid out the basics of customer segmentation and provided a general road map to doing it for your practice. The key, of course, is that you must have the data to determine a successful segmentation strategy. We hope that this chapter motivates you to take a data-oriented view of your practice. Segmentation and the ability to properly target clients require it.

In the next chapter, we focus on the segments that FAs typically target. We focus on segments and niches that have proven to be valuable and discuss what must be done to target them successfully.

NOTES

1. G. A. Moore, *Crossing the Chasm: Marketing and Selling High-Tech Products to Mainstream Customers* (New York: Harper Business, 1991).

2. People sometime use Amazon.com as an example; however, Amazon.com uses collaborative filtering, which is not exactly one-to-one marketing, and also in many quarters of its operation it has not been profitable.

3. V. Mahajan, E. Mueller, and Y. Wind, "A Choice-Based Approach to the Diffusion of a Service: Forecasting Fax Penetration by Market Segments," *Marketing Science* 11, no. 1 (Winter 2000), 39–53.

4. R. B. Cattell, "The Scree Test for the Number of Factors," *Multivariate Behavioral Research* 1 (1966), 245–276.

5. B. Schwartz, *The Paradox of Choice: Why More Is Less* (New York: Ecco, 2004).

6. Fredrick Webster, *Industrial Marketing Strategy*, 3rd ed. (New York: John Wiley & Sons, 1991). See also http://en.wikipedia.org/wiki/Industrial_market_segmentation for an excellent summary of segmentation.

7. J. S. Armstrong, "The Value of Formal Planning for Strategic Decisions," *Strategic Management Journal* 3 (1982), 197–211.

8. Jakob Nielsen, "The Use and Misuse of Focus Groups," *IEEE Software* 14, no. 1 (January/ February 1997), 94.

CHAPTER 3

REFINING YOUR NICHE STRATEGY

A theme that clearly emerges from the modern marketing approach is that one size does *not* fit all. Clients and prospects vary dramatically in their behaviors, demographics, psychographics, benefits sought, investable assets, and many other variables. Now that you have a good understanding of the segmentation, targeting, and positioning process, this chapter seeks to go more deeply into the segments and niches that are most attractive to financial advisors. We need to emphasize that the decision to pursue one segment over another does not rest solely on the perceived attractiveness of that segment alone. Our strong view is that you should target a segment that is both attractive *and* a good match with your individual strengths. This idea will be discussed further in Chapter 4, on branding.

We believe that a segmentation strategy is critical to long-term success, as we make clear in Chapter 2. The diversity of clients and the seemingly infinite variety of investment vehicles available make being a true generalist nearly impossible. How can you believably be the expert on helping newly retired individuals create a long-term income plan, while also being the go-to advisor for wealthy young entrepreneurs? Moreover, managing wealth has become more complex, as clients are seeking out an ever-expanding variety of investment vehicles. Beyond traditional plans that use equities, fixed income, and cash, investors are increasingly becoming interested in REITs, commercial and investment real estate, commodities, private equity, hedge funds, foreign currency, socially responsible investing, green investing, and so on. Add in tax implications and difficult economic times, and it is too much for one individual advisor to do well. The answer is to specialize. Either individually or within a team practice, you must identify a segment that matches your strengths and tailor a marketing mix to that segment. We strongly believe that advisors with a clear target segment are at an advantage over advisors who pursue anybody and everybody who wants to invest with them.

Of the advisors we surveyed, only 61 percent reported having a target segment of clients. We believe that this is too low, and evidence suggests that advisors with a well-articulated target segment are more successful over the long term. The most common segments identified in our survey were high-net-worth (HNW) individuals, the at-retirement market, and small business owners. While classifying clients as HNW and at-retirement narrows down the market somewhat, we consider these to be sectors that have more refined segments or niches within them. In addition to small business owners, advisors identified narrower niches such as nonprofit organizations and their employees, employees of particular school districts, employees and executives of individual companies, specific ethnic groups, and specific groups of professionals. We will break down these sectors and niches in the following pages.

THE HIGH-NET-WORTH SECTOR

Despite the economic turmoil of the last few years, the high-net-worth (HNW) sector has continued to grow. The World Wealth Report,[1] put out annually by Merrill Lynch and Capgemini, shows an expanding number of HNW individuals who control a growing amount of assets in 2008. The affluent market (commonly defined as US$500,000 or more in investable assets), the HNW market (commonly defined as US$1 million or more in investable assets), and the ultra-HNW market (commonly defined as US$30 million or more in investable assets) have been consistently expanding and are expected to continue to grow. There has been particularly vigorous growth in Brazil, Russia, India, China, and the Middle East. Specifically, the report shows that in 2007:

- There are 3.3 million HNW individuals in North America (a 4.2 percent increase over 2006) worth US$11.7 trillion (a 4.4 percent increase over 2006).

- There are 10.1 million HNW individuals worldwide (a 6 percent increase over 2006) worth US$40.7 trillion (a 9.4 percent increase over 2006).

- Predicted annual growth in North America is 6.8 percent to US$16.3 trillion by 2012.

- Predicted annual growth globally is 7.7 percent to US$59.1 trillion by 2012.

In the uncertain markets of the mid- to late 2000s, HNW investors made moves toward safer investments, including fixed income, cash, and domestic markets. Furthermore, the Phoenix Wealth Survey showed that investors were equally split on whether preservation of assets or return on investment was the more important investment goal.[2] It is expected that these investors will move back toward riskier allocations as the economy turns more positive. Despite uncertain markets and a shift toward more conservative allocations, the Phoenix Wealth Survey indicated that HNW investors remained optimistic, with 56 percent feeling that their long-term wealth is extremely secure and 81 percent reporting that they feel more wealthy than last year.

Another trend revealed in the World Wealth Report was an increased interest among HNWs in green investing. In addition to the clear growth opportunities, increased awareness of global warming and related political and environmental concerns have driven more money into alternative fuels, solar energy, and wind technology. This trend is especially prevalent in Asia and the Middle East.

Differences among HNW Investors

The HNW sector is made up of several niches and can be subsegmented in a variety of ways. HNW investors are extremely heterogeneous and should not be expected to always share the same goals, values, and investment approaches. Even if you are exclusively targeting clients with a certain amount of investable assets, a thorough client profile is necessary to determine if there is a good match between you and a prospect. You must consider the prospect's individual needs and goals as well as variables such as his wealth band, age, source of wealth, cultural differences, and so on.

The most common approach is to segment clients by wealth band, or the amount of their investable assets. Ultra-HNW investors, for instance, are much more likely to be interested in alternative investments and passion investments than HNW and affluent investors.[3] Also, ultra-HNWs tend to have more than one advisor and look to particular advisors for their specialized expertise and advice or their ability to play a managing role for multiple advisors. This is an opportunity to get your foot in the door and eventually get a larger dollar share from those clients. While some distinctions exist based on amount of wealth, and advising certainly becomes more complex when bigger amounts of money are involved, segmenting on wealth alone is probably not sufficient.

Another way to segment is by age. The 2007 Phoenix Wealth Survey shows that younger HNW investors are more concerned with maintaining their wealth than baby boomers are. Despite having more money at a younger age than previous HNW generations, they are more concerned with economic downturns, health-care costs, caring for aging parents, and their own longevity. Although many have acquired their wealth through technology and entrepreneurialism, advisors consistently report that this group is surprisingly conservative and concerned with protecting assets.

Cultural differences can also be at the root of differences in behavior. For example, HNW investors from Asia tend to have acquired their wealth entrepreneurially and have less experience with wealth management. In contrast, HNWs of Middle Eastern origins tend to have inherited wealth and are often concerned with compliance with Islamic law when investing. Many advisors working with Eastern European HNWs report a particular interest in passion investments and status items such as art, jewelry, luxury vehicles, and luxury consumables such as wine.

We have personally taught seminars for HNW investors and found them to be incredibly diverse. For example, at one event, we talked with three unadvised investors who had three completely different concerns and expectations of advisors. The first investor was very conservative and, as amazing as it sounds, had all of his money in bonds. He complained of not being able to find an advisor who did not make him feel stupid for being so risk-averse. The second investor wanted an advisor who would help him find socially responsible investments and so-called blue, or politically liberal, investments. He and his wife were unhappy with potential advisors who did not respect their strong beliefs and incorporate their values into an investment plan. The third investor was clearly looking to expand his wealth rapidly and aggressively and wanted an advisor who was experienced with foreign markets and alternative investments. While these three investors all shared similar demographics and amounts of investable assets (in the tens of millions), each was looking for something different in an advisor. In Chapter 5, we will discuss further the importance of discovering and understanding differing individual clients' needs.

Marketing to HNWs

While you must recognize the many differences within the HNW sector, our survey of advisors and discussions with HNW investors themselves reveal some common themes:

- *Relationships.* Trust and advocacy are of utmost importance to the HNW client. A Cogent Research[4] study of HNW investors reveals understanding of needs, instilling a sense of control, clear articulation of fee structure, and taking responsibility as key drivers of satisfaction with advisors. Among investors without an advisor, lack of trust was listed as a primary reason for going it alone. Of those indicating a lack of trust, 94 percent claimed that advisors do not have their best interests at heart.

- *Value proposition.* While important with every type of client, a clearly articulated value proposition is necessary to even open the door with HNW clients. Investors in the Cogent Research study listed choosing the best products for their goals, advisor knowledge, and receiving the best possible advice for the fees charged as the most important responsibilities of an advisor. Among nonadvised investors, confidence in managing their own investments and advisors not providing enough value were listed as the top two reasons for not employing an advisor.

- *Skepticism.* HNW investors are discerning in their assessment of their advisor's expertise. They are skeptical of advisors who seem to be expert in everything. Many times investors are looking for a wealth planner or a personal CFO who can tap into specific expertise when necessary. This is where a team practice or access to the global resources of a multinational firm can be leveraged.

- *Communication.* Proactive communication and problem resolution are of particular importance to HNWs. By reaching out with new ideas, alerts, and clarification of fees, you are sending the signal that you are thinking about them and putting their needs first. The Phoenix Wealth Survey reveals that over 40 percent of HNWs reported some dissatisfaction with advisors proactively maintaining contact, and this was listed as the most common reason for switching advisors. In additional studies and anecdotes, proactive communication consistently emerges as one of the most important determinants of retention. As we discuss in Chapter 7, retention is a key aspect of long-term success.

- *Marketing materials.* HNW clients have little time for or patience with mass communications. They generally do not pay attention to nonspecialized newsletters and nonpersonalized letters. They are more receptive to customized communications that pertain directly to their interests and needs. For instance, original research and white papers that address an issue that is relevant to a particular individual are much better received and more likely to be read.

- *Seminars.* HNW clients are increasingly receptive to seminars and educational events, but these must have clear value. As with written materials, these offerings must be specific to the needs of the audience. In the Phoenix Wealth Survey, HNW investors indicated that seminars on specific wealth-management strategies and estate planning were the most likely to spark their interest. Also, younger HNW investors were more interested in seminars than are older investors. This is also an area where Webinars might be of value as the technology becomes more sophisticated.

Clearly, there are huge and growing opportunities among the HNWs. Trends show that HNW investors are moving away from brokers toward full-service advisors and planners. Also, HNW clients tend to be generally satisfied and loyal to their advisors, making them valuable targets. However, these positives attract intense competition and make these investors hard to acquire. Therefore, if you are to compete, you must not only understand the profiles and trends of HNW investors, but also have a target within the sector and a clear means for communicating your points of differentiation. Investment products are increasingly seen as commodities, especially among HNW investors. This underscores the importance of understanding your target segment and creating real points of differentiation.

THE AT-RETIREMENT SECTOR

Several financial services companies have recently repositioned themselves as "retirement specialists," and for good reason. In the United States alone, 79 million baby boomers are beginning to enter retirement. Compared to previous generations, baby boomers will be in retirement for a much longer time, some for over 40 years. Not only does this demographic have huge needs for investment and planning advice, but these people will also need retirement income and spending strategies, as defined-contribution plans are playing an ever-increasing role. This generational wave has created a sea change of opportunity for retirement planning and wealth management.

Attitudes and Knowledge

While optimism and confidence in enjoying a comfortable retirement have been riding high for years, the recent turbulent economic conditions have reduced these positive feelings. The nonpartisan Employee Benefit Research Institute (EBRI)[5] has found that retirement worries are growing. The percentage of workers who are very confident about having enough for a comfortable retirement has dropped to 18 percent in 2008. Among current retirees, only 29 percent are very confident of having a financially secure retirement. Health-care issues dominate retirees' concerns, with 44 percent saying that they pay more for health care than they had expected and 54 percent saying that they are more concerned with health-care costs than they were before they retired. This study, as well as others, shows eroding confidence in social security and other entitlements among both the working and the retired. These trends promise to get worse before they get better. Despite these pessimistic attitudes and current economic turmoil, other studies such as the AXA Equitable Retirement Scope[6] show that people continue to associate retirement with concepts such as freedom, travel, and rest much more than with negatives such as death or loneliness.

Causing further concern is the modest level of retirement-related financial literacy. The MetLife Retirement Income IQ Study shows that respondents consistently underestimate their longevity, preretirement benchmarks for income, health-care costs, and long-term-care costs. Also, they overestimate retirement savings withdrawal percentages. For instance, a full 43 percent believed that they could withdrawal 10 percent or more annually while preserving their principal. Adding to the problem is the fact that simply too few people are adequately planning for their retirement early enough. The EBRI study showed that only 47 percent of workers have tried to calculate the amount of money they will need for retirement and only 64 percent are currently saving for retirement at all.

While some of these figures are head-shaking, they highlight the opportunities that exist for advisors, both now and in the future. Many of these studies, when compared to figures from just a few years ago, show that people are waking up to the looming retirement crisis and are becoming more aware of their need to take action.

Retirement Phases and Types

As we have discussed, at-retirement is a huge market and not merely a client segment. There is a great deal of heterogeneity among these millions of people. One way to break down the at-retirement market is to analyze the phases of retirement and types of retirees. One thing to recognize is that retirement is a longer process than it was in the past. Many people no longer have a firm date for retirement and are likely to ease into the process. In addition, retirees are more active and are living longer than ever before.

One longitudinal look at the retirement process is offered in the New Retirement Mindscape study.[7] This study revealed that there are five distinct phases of retirement:

- *Imagination.* This stage begins 6 to 15 years before retirement and is marked by high expectations. More than two-thirds of respondents report having high expectations for adventure in retirement, yet only

44 percent report feeling that they are financially on track. This gap represents a marketing opportunity for advisors to help resolve the stated discrepancy between high expectations and actual savings.

- *Anticipation.* During the five years prior to retirement, optimism rises as people anticipate their life after retirement. During this phase, 91 percent expect to be happy in retirement, and 81 percent believe that they will achieve their dreams. Despite all this optimism, only 62 percent have calculated their required retirement income, and only 40 percent have a formal financial plan in place. The primary cause of anxiety at this stage is paying for health care, with 35 percent identifying it as the hardest thing they will have to deal with.

- *Liberation.* This is the implementation phase, which lasts for the first year or so of retirement. Around 80 percent report enjoying themselves and feeling busy. This is the time when people are most likely to have a financial advisor, with 45 percent reporting that they have an advisor and 44 percent reporting that they have a plan.

- *Reorientation.* After their initial enthusiasm for their new life wanes, people report some readjustment and begin to divide into different groups. A fifth of retirees become the so-called *reinventors*, who take charge of their retirement and are highly engaged in work, travel, and hobbies. They feel empowered by the freedom that retirement brings, and they embrace new adventures and new challenges. Another fifth, the *contents*, are very happy but much less adventurous. They are seemingly carefree and happy to let things unfold easily in retirement. In contrast, about 22 percent are still trying to figure things out. These people, the *searchers*, report ambivalent feelings about this stage and are less likely than the previous two groups to have planned for retirement and are less likely to feel financially secure. The remaining 40 percent are the *strugglers*. These people are least likely to feel happy, with only 31 percent reporting that they are enjoying retirement. Also, they are most likely to report feeling depressed, empty, worried, and bored. These are the people who are least likely to have planned for retirement.

- *Reconciliation.* At around 15 years, retirement is seen as a time for coming to terms. People are relatively happy and content at this stage, but health concerns can intervene. There is also an increased concern with inheritance and estate matters, with 75 percent valuing advice on the topic.

Other findings from this study reinforce the importance of the advisor relationship. Results suggest that an advisor has just as important an impact on emotions and fulfillment as she does on feelings of financial preparedness. Those who have an advisor tend to have more optimism, have higher expectations, and ultimately be more fulfilled in retirement than those who are unadvised. Financial advisors (FAs) clearly play a vital and important role in this sector.

Other segmentations of retirees show that there are distinct styles of retirement. For instance, there are six identifiable retirement types based on a retiree's emotional approach and level of activity[8]:

- *Continuers,* who continue to use their skills and pursue lifelong interests
- *Adventurers,* who seek out new challenges, such as businesses and education
- *Searchers,* who explore new options on a trial-and-error basis, but have planned things out less than the previous two groups
- *Easy gliders,* who let the days unfold without much planning at all
- *Involved spectators,* who maintain old interests at a much lighter pace and from a different perspective
- *Retreaters,* who are unhappy and retreat from life

There are other ways to divide up the at-retirement market beyond the two we have discussed, but the message is that there are big differences among retirees, as is true of any large market. While your point of differentiation may be your expertise on retirement issues, that does not mean that at-retirement is your niche. You must segment within this group and understand that different phases, amounts of investable assets, demographics, and emotional types require different approaches and marketing mixes.

WOMEN

Female investors are growing in importance and garnering more and more attention from the financial services industry. As women are earning more and becoming increasingly independent, the amount of assets under their control has also grown. A 2008 Prudential study revealed that a majority of women are solely or jointly responsible for IRAs and other investments.[9] Additionally, more than 75 percent feel that they need help making financial decisions, while only 40 percent feel that they are on track with their retirement savings. The AXA Equitable Retirement Scope reveals that only 50 percent of retired women feel that they have an adequate income, compared to 77 percent of men.[10] These findings are consistent with many others showing that women lag behind men in financial preparedness. These data further suggest that women are very concerned with their financial situations and are potentially more receptive to professional financial advice.

While it is difficult to consider women a niche, given that they represent half of the population, many advisors have found success by making women feel comfortable in an area that has traditionally been male-dominated. In this sense, specializing in serving women becomes a point of differentiation. Advisors who regularly work with women report that relationships, partnership, and education are the keys to successfully serving these investors. Advisors in our programs have indicated that a longer process and a more holistic approach are necessary. Female investors are reluctant to simply turn over decision making to a heavy-handed advisor. They want to be part of the process and to be educated along the way. The Prudential study supports these views, suggesting that planning and guidance have a positive impact on female investors' confidence. Women in the study put a high premium on knowledge and education from social networks, including advisors. This suggests that a more personalized branding approach makes sense.

OTHER SEGMENTS AND NICHES

When teaching marketing to financial advisors, we spend quite a bit of time discussing the advantages of pursuing specific niches. We also solicit insights from successful advisors on their niche strategies. Here are some of the most attractive niches identified by advisors in our studies:

- *Small business owners.* The typical affluent or HNW client today is likely to be an entrepreneur. Because these people are in control of their businesses, they feel a great deal of responsibility for other people. They feel that their family, as well as their employees, partners, and investors, also shares in the risks of their business. Therefore, their family is of central concern when they think about asset protection, risk management, and retirement planning. They also require additional expertise on retirement, disability income protection, and health care because they often do not have company plans or are responsible for providing these benefits themselves.

- *Endowments and trusts.* The management of family and organizational endowments and trusts is a growing segment. One of the key differences with this segment is the decision-making units with which you must deal. Usually there are several family members or a board that hires and works with advisors. The people who are making the decisions are not necessarily knowledgeable, which again calls for an education and partnership approach. Also, goals may vary. For organizations, an endowment is a resource to help them accomplish a social mission. For families, it can mean a legacy that will carry on for generations. In both cases, asset protection and risk management are the overriding concerns.

- *Professionals.* Many FAs we have worked with have found success by specializing in advising clients who work in a certain profession, such as physicians, lawyers, or real estate agents. When you become an expert on the unique income patterns, challenges, and benefits of a certain profession, you differentiate yourself from your competition and create value for your clients. Furthermore, professional clients are well connected and often are trusted advisors to others whom they serve, making them strategically valuable to you. Real estate agents are a particularly good example. They are usually independent businesspeople who have widely varying incomes, sometimes having tens of thousands of dollars to invest at once and other times having nothing. They are also not likely to have company benefits. This all requires a unique planning approach that is tailored to their needs. While this requires extra effort, real estate agents are highly networked and know many people who are moving into an area. They regularly recommend other service providers to their clients, making them a good source for referrals.

- *Ethnic, religious, and cultural groups.* As we will discuss in further depth in Chapter 5, people are more likely to choose an advisor from a group to which they belong than someone who is not apparently affiliated with them in any obvious way. We naturally trust people like ourselves more than we trust people who are perceived to be dissimilar. If you are a member of a particular ethnic or cultural group, this is a good source of prospects. If you are a member of such a group, then you are familiar with its cultural differences, values, and norms. Many advisors we have worked with have created successful practices by catering to the needs of an ethnic, cultural, or religious community within a certain geographic area and becoming the go-to advisor for that group.

- *Nonprofit employees.* Like small business owners, people working in the nonprofit sector have unique needs associated with their compensation and benefits packages. They also have chosen their profession based on certain values. An advisor who understands these unique needs and values will have a distinct advantage with these clients. Furthermore, this is a growing segment with increasing salaries.

- *Employees of individual companies, universities, and school districts.* Again, this is a chance to have expertise with a particular group that is clearly superior to that of your competition. For example, we know an FA who works exclusively with employees at our university. He knows our compensation packages, retirement plans, and benefits better than our HR people do. This makes him an invaluable asset to the people he advises. He anticipates the employees' needs by identifying gaps in their benefits, while creating credibility by not trying to duplicate benefits that they already have. Advisors who have intimate knowledge of a particular company, university, or school district can build a good client base within that group by providing expert knowledge and synergistic solutions.

CONCLUSION

We believe the benefits of a niche strategy are clear. By drilling down into a niche, you are leveraging your strengths, reinforcing your points of differentiation, adding value for your clients, and maximizing your chances of getting referrals. We have discussed several segments and niches in which advisors have found success. By focusing on a niche, you are not limiting your market; you are maximizing your chances of success.

NOTES

1. Capgemini and Merrill Lynch, "World Wealth Report 2008"; http://www.ml.com/media/100472.pdf.
2. 2007 Phoenix Wealth Survey.
3. Capgemini and Merrill Lynch, "World Wealth Report 2008."
4. Barclays Global Investors, *Measuring Affluent and HNW Investor Expectations of the Investment and Financial Community*, report prepared by Cogent Research for iShares, March 2008.
5. Employee Benefit Research Institute, *2008 Retirement Confidence Survey*, EBRI Issue Brief 316, April 2008.
6. AXA Equitable, *AXA Equitable Retirement Scope: New Dynamics*, February 2008.
7. Ameriprise Financial, in conjunction with Age Wave, Ken Dychtwald, and Harris Interactive, Inc., *New Retirement Mindscape*, 2006.

8. Nancy K. Schlossberg, *Retire Smart, Retire Happy: Finding Your True Path in Life* (Washington, D.C.: American Psychological Association, 2004).

9. Prudential Financial, *Financial Experience and Behaviors among Women*, 2008–2009.

10. AXA Equitable, *AXA Equitable Retirement Scope.*

CHAPTER 4

KNOWING YOUR BRAND

In this chapter, we will cover the basics of building a strong brand for your financial advisory practice. You may be thinking that you can't afford a brand, since you are not a major corporation with billions of dollars to invest in advertising. But whether you know it or not, you already have one. One way to think about your brand is this: your brand is your reputation. One of your most important assets is your reputation. That is, what concepts do clients and prospects associate with you? You must know that you *are* a brand. You must treat your reputation like a brand by investing in it, protecting it, cultivating it, and leveraging it.

You will pay a high price for thinking that you don't have a brand or that you don't need one. Too often, financial advisors try to be everything to everyone. Yet if they took a more targeted approach that concentrated on their brands and the strongest part of their brands, they could net better results. A strong brand built on a foundation of differentiation from the competition and burnished with constant reinforcement of that image is more than a fundamental building block. Financial advisors with strong brands have higher market share, charge higher prices, and collect higher margins. This is also known as "triple jeopardy" in the marketing literature. It is somewhat counterintuitive because many advisors erroneously believe that higher prices lead to lower share.

WHAT IS A BRAND?

The American Marketing Association (AMA) says that a brand is "a name, term, design, symbol or any other feature that identifies one seller's good or service as distinct from those of other sellers." And while you might think that the AMA knows what it's talking about, when it comes to financial advisory services, this seems like an inadequate definition. No doubt the AMA got a bunch of marketers together in a room, and they decided to stick to the most basic definition of a brand: your name or your logo. While we might all agree that a cow marked with a triple C or interlocking diamonds belongs to one rancher rather than another, we know that branding means far more than that to good marketers.

In our survey of FAs, we have asked, "What does branding mean to you?" many times, and we have gotten many answers. We've heard answers like, "No idea what it is referring to," or, "The latest marketing term," suggesting that this FA didn't think much of the concept. Others, echoing the American Marketing Association, have suggested that branding is "creating a logo" or "what cowboys do." Others who have given the idea a little more thought have suggested that branding is, "Creating 'top of mind awareness' in our clients' minds regarding a particular service," or, "When the public thinks of a product or service, your name comes to mind." These answers are characteristic of the most common set of replies to our question. They all suggest that a brand is just about being at the top of a customer or client's mind.

This is a better definition than the one provided by the AMA. At least it gets at the idea that brands and branding have an impact on what consumers think, and presumably on the choices they make. Many marketers, when creating a brand-building strategy, will focus on generating more awareness for their brand as the key measure of success. Certainly strong brands have high levels of awareness among their target markets. If consumers don't know that the brand exists, they are unlikely to ever consider buying it. This set of considered brands is called the *consideration set* and is shown to be a primary driver of brand choice. But most of you are probably very aware of many brands that you have never considered buying and never will. Knowing that something exists doesn't mean that you like it or want it. Awareness is a necessary, but not sufficient, condition for building a brand in the marketplace.

So, if branding isn't just building awareness, what else is it? Looking at the responses to our FA survey, we see answers like, "A sense of who we are that rises above just our company name and/or logo," and, "It means what the client thinks of you." These replies suggest that branding is more than what the AMA's definition implies and more than just being sure that consumers are aware of you. Consumers not only are aware of strong brands, but understand what those brands offer and how the brands are relevant to their own needs. Strong brands have high rates of awareness, but they go beyond being top of mind to being *meaningful* for clients. So, what does it mean to be meaningful?

At the most basic level, consumers should know what the brand does and what makes it unique in the marketplace. As one of our survey respondents put it, my brand is, "What identifies/distinguishes me and my practice. For example, Honda equals quality and low cost of ownership. The Home Depot equals homebuilders' repair and remodel solutions." When clients think of the brand, key associations should come to mind. Ideally, the associations should be characterized by three features[1]:

- They should be *strong*. Your clients shouldn't have to think too hard in order to come up with what they think of your brand. These associations should be easily generated. Not only should the brand name be top of mind, but what it stands for should be top of mind as well. We discuss top-of-mind words (your "three words") later in the book.

- Hopefully, the associations are also *favorable*, rather than unfavorable.

- Lastly, these associations should be *unique*. The associations that clients can generate for your brand should be different from the associations that they might generate for a competitive brand.

At the same time, though, branding is more than what marketers themselves do; branding is *how clients perceive the brand*. Ultimately, a brand is a psychological construct;

something that exists in the minds of your clients. Your brand, then, is what your clients perceive it to be.[2] Of course, you influence what they think through the name and logo you choose, the products and services you offer, the ways in which you deliver those products and services, and everything else you do.

But client associations with your brand also reflect your clients' own idiosyncratic perceptions. These perceptions can come from anywhere—from the media, from their friends (a very strong influence), from family members or colleagues, from broader cultural influences, or from their own moment-to-moment thoughts and feelings as they consider your brand. Different clients interacting with the same brand will often have quite different sets of associations concerning that brand. Some of these might be shared across clients, while others will be unique. And very often, those associations are different from what the marketer, or you, might expect or want them to be. A very salient and real example from 2003, described next, highlights this.

In early 2003, a group of Merrill Lynch HR employees came to Wharton for an educational program. As part of that program, they were asked to write down the "first three things that come to mind" when they think of Merrill Lynch. The HR employees generated associations like "Five Principles," "Employee Opportunities," "Global," and "The Bull," which usually led to other associations like "Big," "Powerful," and "Strong." These Merrill Lynch employees also asked the same question of friends and neighbors who did not work for Merrill Lynch and reported their answers back. This was definitely not a scientific sample, yet it offers an example of how internal company associations can be quite different from external associations. Those outside respondents, some of them Merrill Lynch clients, said things like, "The Bull," "American Company," and, interestingly, "Martha Stewart." Not one of the employees mentioned Martha Stewart, but nearly all the nonemployee respondents did.

At the time, Martha Stewart, the founder of the media company, was being investigated for potential insider trading, which was done, allegedly, with the involvement of her Merrill Lynch advisor. She had not yet been indicted for lying to investigators or put on trial in the same courtroom as her advisor. Yet, for a time at least, when many consumers thought of Merrill Lynch, they also thought of Martha Stewart. In the short term, the likelihood that this association was made probably went up, as Martha and her advisor went on trial and her haircuts, outfits, and handbags dominated the news night after night. For a while, it was probably a strong association, one that was uniquely associated with Merrill Lynch relative to its competitors, but unfortunately, not one that was terribly favorable. Today, it's likely that very few consumers would associate Martha Stewart with the Merrill Lynch brand at all. Associations can fade away, particularly if they aren't reinforced over time. In Merrill Lynch's case, that was probably fortunate for this particular association. But this also suggests that more desirable associations also need tending and reinforcement over time if they are to remain stuck in clients' minds.

This Merrill Lynch example also illustrates another issue: where do clients get information about your brand? Revisiting our survey, one particular FA answered the question about what his brand means by responding, "What my clients know about my parent firm." This is a common answer, especially from younger advisors who feel that their brand rests solely on their corporate affiliation. Another advisor who worked for the same firm answered simply, "Me." This is also a common response. Many advisors think that their corporate affiliation has no impact on their personal brand. These answers are at opposite ends of the spectrum, with one advisor thinking that his brand was wholly driven by what people thought of his firm, while the other felt that her affiliation meant nothing to her clients.

In a sense, both of these answers are correct, and both are wrong. Certainly, your brand does center on you, and it should. In this book, we define *you* as the company, and we are talking about building *your* brand. However, you must recognize that if you are affiliated with a larger firm, clients are going to integrate their view of that firm into their brand associations of you, for better or for worse. If there is a large firm's logo on your card, your clients will pay attention to printed material, e-mail, and ads from that company and associate them with you. Therefore, it is critical that your brand be consistent, or at least not inconsistent, with the messages and image of your parent firm. The associations that clients have with you can come from you, your branch or partnerships, and your large firm affiliations. While you are at the center of your brand, clients will integrate information from all of these sources. We refer to this as the *branding umbrella* (Figure 4.1).

We can also think of a brand's meaning beyond just the associations that a client or potential client might generate. At a deeper level, the brand's meaning might reflect how the client views the brand as relevant to his goals or objectives. A client might understand what a particular FA offers in terms of products and services, and might also understand how that FA is differentiated from others. These associations might

Figure 4.1 You Are at the Center of the Branding Umbrella

indeed even possess strength, favorability, and uniqueness. But none of that will matter if the client doesn't think that those things are relevant to his life. You'd like your brand to represent a path, or opportunity, by which clients can achieve their own goals. In many ways, this is the ultimate client-focused definition of branding. You would like your brand meaning to reflect the client's goals and aspirations.

Earlier, we said that your brand is what your clients perceive it to be. Now we are going beyond that. We are saying that your brand is what your clients think they can accomplish if they partner with you. When your practice stands for that, you have the opportunity to *transcend* a brand based on awareness and associations and to create a brand that offers the opportunity to build long-term relationships. In the personal realm, we don't build relationships with people we have heard of and know a bit about. We may start there, but ultimately we build relationships with people who we believe can be true partners in our own endeavors. Who wouldn't want to be thought of as a partner by her clients? It's equally true in the branding world. Implicit in this is the notion that no brand can help every client or customer accomplish every kind of goal. To make this more explicit, it means that you have to focus on making sure that the right clients are aware of you, on creating associations for the *right* clients, and on demonstrating that you can help a *certain segment of clients* to achieve their goals. You must make sure that for those clients, but not for others, you will be the right FA for them to establish a long-term relationship with. This should sound very familiar if you've read the previous two chapters on segmentation and selecting a niche market.

A nice way to think hierarchically about developing your brand is the four-point outline described in Figure 4.2. You might think of this as a "ladder of branding." If you are to help your clients climb to the top, they have to start out on the awareness rung, but that alone is not enough. Your marketing and branding activities need to support the process

Figure 4.2 Ladder of Branding

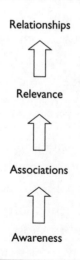

Relationships

Relevance

Associations

Awareness

of stepping up the ladder to build associations, or meaning, in the client's mind.

Near the top of the ladder comes not just knowledge of what the brand does and how it does it, but an understanding of how the brand fits into the client's life—that is, how the brand is relevant to the client's goals and aspirations, and how it can help the client achieve them. Once a client sees how you and your brand are relevant to his own personal goals, he can begin to consider your brand as a relationship partner and potentially step up to the very top of the ladder. This is when clients increase their assets under management, feel loyalty, and recommend you.

These relationships are the pinnacle of strong brands, and they are often based on an emotional connection between the brand and the client. The pinnacle of branding comes when it replicates a human relationship, complete with the emotional connections that humans have when they are close to one another. Consumer packaged goods companies spend millions of dollars trying to create that emotional connection between their brands and their clients (consumers). There's a difference between clients buying a product out of habit and true loyalty. Both might lead to clients making repeat purchases, but the depth of commitment is different. Apple users don't use the brand because it's a habit. They are fiercely loyal to the brand, often choosing it in the face of obstacles like higher prices, incompatibility, and limited software titles. As in human relationships, the emotions in consumer-brand relationships reflect an implicit contract: partners expect certain benefits from the relationship, but they are also committed to support the other partner and are vested in the other partner's success. Compared to the consumer packaged goods companies that are trying to create these types of relationships, FAs have an advantage because they are well practiced in building and maintaining human relationships. Your natural capabilities can help you move up the branding ladder to develop relationships with your clients, but it's important to remember that these relationships rest on a foundation of awareness, associations, and relevance to the client's objectives.

DIFFERENTIATING YOUR BRAND

So, how do you actually create a brand that reaches the top of that ladder? First, you need to understand that if your brand represents all the perceptions that clients have of you, then *everything* you do (and everything your parent firm, partners, and staff do) can influence those perceptions. Thus, everything you do is branding. As one of our survey respondents put it, branding is "marketing everything about you and your practice with a consistent theme, which includes, but is not limited to, company logo, expertise of the firm, and advertising. Branding is all that goes into making a client in your niche think of you and your firm to help solve his problems." This is one of the best and most complete definitions of branding we have seen.

Let's pick up on the point that this respondent mentioned about having a consistent theme. How do you choose such a theme to guide your actions? Your overall marketing strategy should be the theme around which all your branding is organized. Based on your understanding of the five Cs (company, customer, competition, context, and collaborators) that we discussed in Chapter 1, you can implement a strategy that positions your practice to be uniquely relevant, relative to your competitors, to a chosen segment of clients. You might conceptualize that strategy along one of three paths, each representing a particular way of serving the clients you've chosen, as given in Figure 4.3.[3]

Brands that choose to differentiate themselves based on performance superiority are focused on offering leading-edge products and services that consistently push the state of the art. These FA practices are characterized by their "out of the box" culture. Think Apple, which consistently focuses on raising the bar for the iPod and constantly challenging the capabilities of other MP3 players. A financial advisor who is focused on differentiating his or her brand via this path will probably offer clients access to the most innovative financial products on the market, the most functional Web site where clients can access information about their accounts, and perhaps even a steady stream of seminars to educate clients about the characteristics of these

Figure 4.3 Different Ways of Branding Your Practice

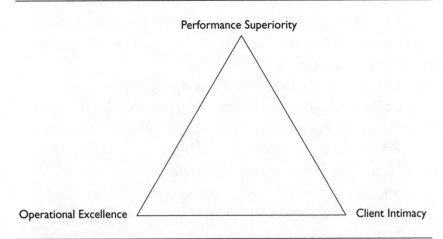

innovative financial products. In all decisions, the FA will focus on delivering a steady stream of innovative products and services to clients.

Brands that choose to differentiate themselves based on operational excellence are focused on leading the market on pricing and/or convenience, and do so with remarkable consistency and reliability. Think McDonald's, which has perfected the art of delivering the same quality of service at reasonable prices in every location around the globe. While these companies often deliver exceptional value for a low price, they are not necessarily always the low-price leader. Sometimes they are actually priced relatively high in terms of economic prices, but offer lower "psychological" prices by being the easiest to interact with, the most convenient, or the most reliable. Think of FedEx, which isn't usually the low-cost leader in express package delivery, but is seen as the leader when it comes to convenience and reliability. These companies are characterized by a "one size fits all" culture, which allows them to focus on achieving economies and efficiencies that they can then pass along to their customers. A financial advisor who focuses on differentiation via this path will probably offer clients consistent, transparent pricing on a set of off-the-shelf products and services that would be appropriate for most clients with little customization.

Brands that choose to differentiate themselves based on customer intimacy are focused on understanding their clients at an individual level and continually exceeding their clients' expectations with truly customized product and service offerings. To succeed, these brands need to develop an obsession for understanding their customers and developing systems for mining, managing, and using the information that they gather.

They are characterized by a flexible, responsive, "have it your way" culture that allows them to provide specific, tailored solutions for their clients rather than more general, off-the-shelf ones. However, brands that make this choice often reject having a large number of potential customers. It is very difficult to know every single customer at the level of detail required for true customization to each of them. Our survey data suggest that at most 75 to 100 clients can truly be managed in this way. A trade-off has to be made between the depth of understanding required for real customization and the number of clients that the brand can serve. These brands focus on the careful selection and nurturance, over a long time horizon, of a smaller slice of the market.

A financial advisor who focuses on differentiating in this way will probably start by targeting a narrow segment of individuals who want unique rather than general solutions to their problems. The FA will focus on delivering a bundle of products and services that can be customized to each particular client, and perhaps to no other. One FA who attended our programs here at Wharton provides an example. This advisor had built a very successful practice focused exclusively on tenured professors in the professional schools (medicine, engineering, business, and law) at a major West Coast university. She differentiated herself with a depth of knowledge about the university's benefit plans and through her unique understanding of the intellectual entrepreneurship that characterized members of her target segment. She knew their research interests and worked to create portfolios for them that reflected the domains they tracked and the values that drove them in both their personal and their professional lives.

This "path model" for differentiation suggests that firms do best when they pick a *single* path. They set themselves apart from the competition with a narrow focus on delivering that one particular value proposition. This is an acknowledgement that it is difficult to be the best in the market at everything. At the same time, it is important not to completely neglect the other two paths. You might offer the most innovative products, but if you are too difficult to do business with or if you have no sense of your clients as individuals, they will forgo your offerings and choose a competitor that offers a better balance. Brands that succeed choose a single path at which they excel and by which they differentiate themselves. However, they also strive for parity on the other two paths.

In nearly every product or service category, you can find brands that focus on delivering value through one of these paths. In the realm of discount retailers, Wal-Mart is clearly the king of the operational excellence model. By focusing on its own internal operational structures, it is able to provide lower prices and greater convenience to its customers. On the other hand, Target pursues a strategy of performance superiority. It relies on cutting-edge designers to deliver goods that are low-priced, although higher-priced than Wal-Mart's, but that also possess a wealth of style and cultural caché. In contrast, Costco seems to have developed a strategy of customer intimacy. Only shoppers who choose to become members are allowed to shop in its stores, where they will find a narrow assortment of alternatives in a much smaller set of product categories than you'd find in either Wal-Mart or Target. Those goods that are available are chosen based on a deep understanding of the Costco shopper and what he will find compelling. Costco isn't the lowest-cost provider, it isn't the most convenient retailer, and it doesn't offer the most cutting-edge style or performance. What it offers is just the right assortment of products at just the right price for its target segment of upper-income, professional suburbanites.

Each of these brands has found remarkable success over time in essentially the same category. This suggests that no one path is necessarily better suited for success than the others. What matters is companywide understanding, commitment, and dedication to delivering on your chosen path as a way to set yourself apart from the competition and deliver to your target clients exactly what they want. Ultimately, choosing which path to pursue comes down to choosing a particular segment of clients that best suits your strengths.

The path you choose should be consistent with what you want your brand to mean to clients. What associations do you want them to have with you? That you're cutting-edge? That you're reliable and easy to do business with? That you know their situations better than they do themselves? In what way do they want you to be relevant to their lives? Because you help them become aware of and maximize their usage of the latest financial products and services? Because you help make it possible for them to manage their money reliably and efficiently, despite their busy personal lives? Or because you help them achieve their unusual goals, given the complexities and uncertainties of their individual situations? The way you answer those questions should give you insight into how to build every aspect of your business to create the right brand image for you in the minds of clients.

BUILDING YOUR BRAND AT EVERY TOUCHPOINT

As we said earlier, if your brand is what your clients perceive it to be, it's important to understand that *everything* that happens drives clients' perceptions. As a result, everything you do potentially undermines or builds your brand. Everything. Not just the financial performance that you achieve for your clients, but everything that happens on the way to achieving that performance. This includes both the consequential and the mundane: the financial plans you create for your clients, the performance those plans achieve, the phone conversations your clients have with your office staff, the pile of correspondence they receive from you (and your parent brand) each month, the coffee you serve when they come in for an annual meeting, and so on. Every aspect of what it's like for a client to interact with you has to be considered for its brand-building or brand-reinforcing potential.

Every FA is focused on creating the appropriate perceptions when she herself is interacting with clients. But what fraction of client time is actually spent directly with you? One way to think about this is to track all the potential touchpoints between your brand and the client. Those touchpoints would include any time the client comes into contact with your brand, whether because you have initiated that contact or because he has initiated it himself. List all the opportunities and each step in every experience in which the client has the potential to interact with, to form an impression of, or to engage with your brand. What is the client doing, thinking, or feeling at each touchpoint? How is your brand currently addressing that experience at each touchpoint?

As an example, take buying a book at Amazon.com. What are all the potential touchpoints between Amazon.com and its customers, and what happens at each one? They actually begin even before the customer arrives at the Amazon.com home page. The first touchpoint might be the moment when the customer considers buying the book and thinks of Amazon.com as a potential source for it. Then perhaps the customer sits down at her computer and types in "Amazon.com." The home page is obviously one of the major touchpoints. How will the client search for the chosen book? By typing something into the search box, or by clicking on a particular category button? Does the customer even have a particular book in mind, or is she just browsing and hoping to come across something interesting? Browsing rather than having a more goal-oriented mindset might lead to a different interaction with Amazon.com overall and a different set of brand-building touchpoints. Does the consumer arrive at just the right item on the first search, or does it take additional, more refined searches? Each of those is a potential touchpoint where Amazon.com can delight or disappoint the customer.

Assuming that the customer finds the right book, the process of placing it into his shopping cart is a touchpoint. If he has finished his shopping, the process of checking out is another touchpoint. The e-mail that Amazon.com sends afterward to confirm the order is a touchpoint. The e-mail sent after that to confirm that the book has been shipped is a touchpoint. The arrival of the box at the customer's home is a touchpoint. How does it look when the customer picks it up? Did it hold up well in the mail? How easy is it to pick up and to open? Does the customer have to dig out his scissors and pry the box open, or can it be opened more easily? The moment of opening the box and seeing the book inside is a touchpoint. How did it fare in the shipping process? Is it packed well? The process of disposing of or recycling the box is a touchpoint. How hard is it to break the box down and dispose of it? Although the shipper might be responsible for some of this, Amazon.com is likely to be held responsible, and it will thus reflect on the company.

The consumption of the actual book is a touchpoint, one that might go on for an extended period of time or that might be experienced multiple times. When the customer talks about the book, and maybe about where she bought it, with a friend or coworker, there is another potential touchpoint with Amazon.com. No doubt there are additional touchpoints in the process that we've overlooked, but you get the picture. If it's this involved and detailed for the process of buying something as commoditized as a book, the touchpoints for buying and consuming financial services are likely to be even more complicated.

Pick a representative client from your client list. What are all the potential touchpoints between that client and your brand over the course of a meaningful time period? Write them all down. Then go back and talk with your team and your staff to make sure you haven't missed any. It will probably be a long list, and most of those touchpoints probably occur outside of your presence. For example, think about how much mail a client gets from you and/or your parent brand. How often does mail with your logo arrive in his mailbox? Mailings, such as statements, confirmations, and disclosures, are often the most frequent touchpoints between an FA and a client. How does the client respond to that mail? Does he know what to do with it? Does he know what is important and what isn't? Does he have a system for organizing the important documents? What are you doing to help manage those touchpoints for your client? Anything? In our sessions, most FAs agree that their clients are inundated with mail related to their financial accounts. Most of them empathize with their clients and are unhappy that because of corporate systems or compliance requirements, the clients are forced to contend with this downpour.

Some, though, go beyond empathy, which *is* important, to develop a strategy to help their clients achieve a better experience when it comes to handling all that mail. For example, one FA we met provides each new client with a large plastic bin branded with her logo, and tells the client to put every piece of mail he gets from the company into that bin. At the end of a month or two, the FA makes an appointment to visit the client's home. She arrives with a binder that again has been branded with her logo and that has already been filled with labeled dividers. She sits down with her client and explains the purpose of each piece of mail, indicating which pieces are important and need to be saved, and which can be shredded or recycled. Then she places the important pieces into the binder for her clients. She leaves the bin and the folder behind and finds that most clients will pick up where she has left off. Once they know which documents need saving and have a system for saving them, they do it themselves. Importantly, not only has the FA helped the client to manage this often overwhelming touchpoint, but by "sitting down on the floor" with the client and sorting through all the mail in the client's home, she has also created an opportunity for the two of them to get to know each other better and to solidify their relationship.

No organization can manage every touchpoint. There will be too many to manage, and some of them might require too great an investment of resources for the returns they will bring (see Chapter 7 for such an analysis where costs outstrip revenues). But you should understand what all those touchpoints are and make deliberate decisions about which of them you will manage and how. You might start with those that are easiest to tackle or those that you think you can best address in a way that is consistent with how you want to build your brand. Alternatively, you might focus on those that you think are the most important to your clients.

Very often, a good place to start is where clients are currently experiencing "points of pain." Where is interacting with your brand more irritating, frustrating, or painful than it should be? There is a substantial amount of academic research, which we will describe in more detail in Chapter 6, showing that small losses can be particularly painful to consumers. These small losses are more painful than small gains or rewards are pleasurable. These points of pain are often associated with the most mundane aspects of consuming a particular product or service. If you've bought a toy for a small child recently, you'll know that the pain associated with prying it out of the package can almost ruin the pleasure of seeing the child happy. Waiting in line can severely impinge on the overall pleasure of that cup of coffee at Starbucks. In contrast, at the Apple store, employees head down the line at the cash register to process credit card transactions via a portable swiper and then send the receipt to your e-mail. A focus on those small points of pain can pay large dividends if they can truly be managed in a way that eliminates or reduces them. The pile of mail that clients receive is an example of a pain point. Once you have made your list of touchpoints, go back and highlight those that are likely to be painful for clients. What could you do to reduce that pain and reinforce your brand meaning in the process?

As you think over your list of touchpoints and make decisions about which of them you will address, it is important to keep in mind *how* you want to address them. Your strategy for addressing each touchpoint should fit with your overall branding strategy. There are many ways to address any one touchpoint, and you want to be sure that your approach is consistent with the brand meaning that you are trying to build. Your strategies should seek to integrate all touchpoints into a cohesive whole that speaks with a single voice to your clients about who you are and what you stand for.

Similarly, it's important that everyone on your team understand her role in building the brand. Everyone who represents your brand needs to understand what the brand-building objectives are, what associations you want to build, and how you want to be perceived. All the members of your team should know what path you have chosen to differentiate yourself in the marketplace. Also, they should constantly be asking themselves if the actions they are taking support that positioning. You may also want to establish evaluation systems that measure how well your team members are fulfilling their brand-building objectives and create compensation mechanisms that reward them for doing so. Building a consistent brand image starts on the inside of the organization, with clarity of objectives and commitment from everyone to fulfill those objectives. Everything in your practice must support the brand you are trying to build.

ARTICULATING YOUR BRAND: THE THREE WORDS

If you were to tell a current or potential client what you offer, how would you do it? Every advisor has heard the admonition to develop the elevator speech, so that you are ready to succinctly articulate who you are and what you offer. In our survey, we've asked FAs to tell us what they say in these speeches—how they try to position themselves in the minds of clients. Nearly every time we've run the survey, a handful of attributes are mentioned by virtually all FAs who respond: (1) I (and my team) have many years of experience, (2) our practice is client-focused, (3) we deliver superior performance, (4) we offer a high level of service to our clients, and (5) I (and my team) have a good reputation and a high level of integrity.

These are all worthy attributes to have. There's only one problem: nearly everyone is claiming them. Everyone is positioning himself in the same way. In our experience, there is virtually no differentiation in the way the majority of FAs present themselves to clients. As a result, these attributes, as worthy as they are, essentially become table stakes. Without them, you can't get a seat at the table. Everyone has to have them, but they don't set you apart from the competition.

So, take those five attributes and set them aside. Think about what you want to stand for in the minds of current and potential clients, and write down three words. Not three sentences, just three words. With those three words, you want to differentiate yourself from your competitors.

You want the words to hang together so that they are consistent with one another. Those three words should reflect the top three associations that you'd like clients to have when they think of you. They are the top three ways in which you are relevant to your clients' goals. The three words should be consistent with the path for differentiating yourself that you've chosen, whether it's operational excellence, performance superiority, or customer intimacy. Boil everything down into this concise statement that differentiates you and reinforces your brand meaning. Once you've identified those three words, go back to your touchpoints and make sure that your actions at each one are consistent with those words. We give some specific examples in Chapter 9 of how successful FAs have expressed their brand and their three words.

In summary, your brand is much more than awareness. Your brand is much more than a set of unrelated tactics. Your brand is much more than you and your team's plans and thoughts about yourselves. A strong brand starts with your strengths and identifies the client segment that matches those strengths. Additionally, a strong brand is consistently reinforced by all the touchpoints and aids in the creation of relationships with clients. Your brand ultimately represents you and your reputation. It is your most valuable asset, and it is the foundation on which you build your business.

NOTES

1. Kevin Lane Keller, *Strategic Brand Management* (Upper Saddle River, N.J.: Prentice Hall, 1998).

2. Kevin Lane Keller, "Conceptualizing, Measuring and Managing Customer-Based Brand Equity." *Journal of Marketing* 57, no. 1 (January 1993), 1–22; Keller, *Strategic Brand Management.*

3. Michael Treacy and Fred Wiersema, *The Discipline of Market Leaders: Choose Your Customers, Narrow Your Focus, Dominate Your Market* (New York: Basic Books, 1997).

CHAPTER 5

THE CLIENT'S DECISION-MAKING PROCESS

In Chapter 1, we outlined the five Cs of marketing strategy: company, clients, competition, collaborators, and context. We emphasized the client C because clients and their referrals are ultimately what drive your profits. The last two chapters have focused on the ways in which clients differ and the different factors that drive their decisions. However, while clients and decisions differ, all clients go through a similar decision-making *process*. In this chapter, we will take you through this process to help you identify the crucial elements that will aid you in attracting, satisfying, and retaining clients.

The client decision-making process is generally broken down into the five steps shown in Figure 5.1.

Figure 5.1 The Client Decision-Making Process

```
┌─────────────────────────────┐
│      Need Recognition        │
└─────────────────────────────┘
                ▼
┌─────────────────────────────┐
│      Information Search       │
└─────────────────────────────┘
                ▼
┌─────────────────────────────┐
│   Evaluation of Alternatives  │
└─────────────────────────────┘
                ▼
┌─────────────────────────────┐
│      Purchase Decision        │
└─────────────────────────────┘
                ▼
┌─────────────────────────────┐
│    Postpurchase Evaluation    │
└─────────────────────────────┘
```

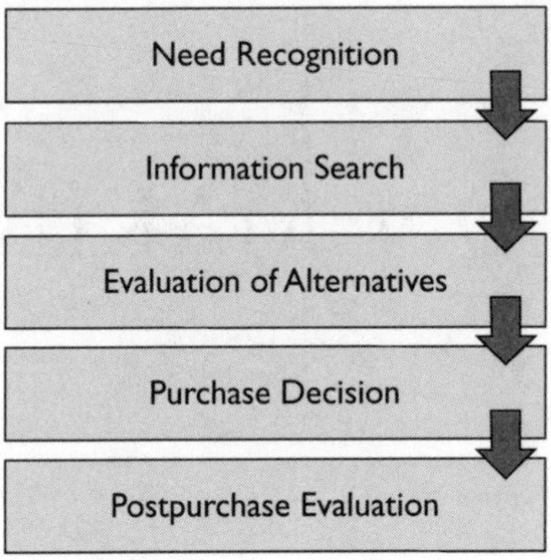

NEED RECOGNITION

Broadly defined, a *need* is a discrepancy between a perceived actual state and a perceived ideal state. For instance, when an individual goes to do laundry and finds that he is out of detergent, that individual recognizes a discrepancy between the actual state (depleted of detergent) and the ideal state (stocked up on detergent). This is where the decision-making process starts: by recognizing a need that the individual is motivated to satisfy. For a financial services client, a broad range of needs emerges: retirement planning, college savings, growing wealth, protecting existing wealth, risk management, tax planning, and so on.

Certainly, most individuals need financial advice; although a huge problem is that many potential clients don't realize this. When you meet with a prospect, a good question protocol (detailed suggestions are found in Chapter 9) can help you identify her specific needs. One of the goals of marketing is to influence the perception of needs by influencing the perceptions of both the actual and the ideal state. In order to influence perception, we first truly have to understand what drives the client's needs and delve deeper into the client's psychology.

In this section, we seek to go beyond the surface-level needs for specific types of products and advice to explore the underlying psychological needs that drive clients' behavior and choices. The field of psychology has investigated needs for decades, and several different models have emerged. Perhaps the best-known approach is Maslow's hierarchy of needs, presented in Figure 5.2.[1]

Maslow's model suggests that there are five levels of needs: physiological needs, such as food, water, and sleep; safety needs, such as security; social needs, such as acceptance and friendship; egoistic needs, such as self-esteem, success, and prestige; and a self-actualization need, which is the need for self-fulfillment. While this approach was originally conceived as a developmental model that would explain how people resolve various crises as they grow and

Figure 5.2 Maslow's Hierarchy of Needs

mature, marketers see value in it for understanding customers' needs. The basic premise of this model is that lower-order needs must be satisfied before higher-order needs can be considered. For example, someone is not usually concerned with satisfying an egoistic need by buying a BMW to impress others if she is worried about the security of her home and family.

This hierarchical approach suggests that advisors need to assess what needs are driving their clients' and prospects' decisions during the initial few meetings. For instance, the discussion of a fulfilling retirement in which one volunteers and travels extensively (self-actualization) is not likely to be motivating to a client who is concerned with protecting his assets for the future of his family (safety). While this approach makes intuitive sense, many advisors make the mistake of trying to satisfy needs that clients are not yet ready to face. However, the strength of Maslow's approach, its simplicity, is also its weakness. It is possible for people to be concerned with needs at multiple levels simultaneously.

A more modern approach to psychological needs suggests that individuals have basic needs that they are motivated to satisfy and that these needs underlie all surface-level needs. Additionally, these needs are not mutually exclusive, meaning that more than one need can motivate a person simultaneously. In other words, these basic needs are always motivating people's actions to some degree and can often overlap. These core needs or motivations are the need for esteem, the need for control, the need for belonging, and the need for meaningfulness (see Figure 5.3).

Figure 5.3 The Four Core Psychological Needs/Motivations

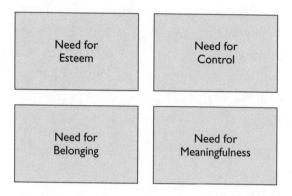

The Need for Esteem

Perhaps no other concept in psychology has been researched as much as self-esteem.[2] Humans are continually motivated to build and maintain positive self-esteem. A search for "self-esteem" on Amazon.com produces more than 120,000 results. The bestseller lists are continually cluttered with guides to building self-esteem. The pursuit of self-esteem manifests itself in many ways, including having unrealistic and optimistic views of ourselves,[3] pursuing success in multiple domains,[4] and the purchase of status symbol items.[5]

Acknowledging clients' need for self-esteem is of utmost importance for two reasons. First, advisors must recognize that personal finance is a self-esteem-threatening experience for many clients. It is intimidating and full of chances to fail, and it also may signal to some clients that they are inadequate because they cannot manage things themselves.

By taking on the role of coach and partner, you have an opportunity to educate and empower your clients. This can turn a self-esteem-threatening situation into a self-esteem-building opportunity. Second, self-esteem can be at the root of what is important about money to some clients. For many people, building wealth is like buying a prestige automobile or an expensive watch. Money becomes a measure of one's self worth.

The Need for Control

While this need is similar to Maslow's safety need, it actually goes much deeper. People want to feel that they are in control of what happens to them. We want to feel that we have an impact on the world around us and that we are not subject to randomness and forces outside of our control. In fact, anxiety is rooted in the feeling of a lack of control and predictability. Simply put, we are very uncomfortable when we perceive our fate to be in the hands of others or, even worse, when we see our fate as completely random.

Lack of control can lead to low self-esteem, and sometimes people go to extreme lengths to restore control or create the illusion of control. Surveys consistently show that investors have a great deal of anxiety about social security, health-care costs, caring for an aging parent, maintaining their lifestyle into retirement, inflation, and other issues that are wholly or partially outside of their direct control. Unfortunately, the typical response for many people is to avoid thinking about these issues by putting off financial planning. Avoidance is one strategy for dealing with potential threats to one's sense of control. People simply will not attend to issues that highlight their lack of control and that produce anxiety.

However, a better way to deal with these issues is to have a sound financial plan that establishes control. Research shows that people differ in their reaction to a loss of control. People with higher levels of optimism and a greater sense of personal control are more likely to use proactive coping mechanisms and face issues directly. In contrast, a generalized poor sense of control is linked to avoidance, poor coping mechanisms, and even self-handicapping behaviors.[6] It is important that you determine your client's sense of control and construct your messages accordingly. Appealing to the anxiety-reducing benefits of having a good long-term plan can often be more powerful than extolling the benefits of particular products.

Another problem is that investors are often reluctant to give up control to an advisor. For many, not having direct control over their investments can be anxiety provoking. It is extremely important that you assess the language you use with prospects and clients to make sure you are building a sense of control with your clients and not inadvertently taking it away. Again, a focus on partnering and education can underscore that your role is to give clients more control over their financial future, not to take it away. Many successful advisors we have worked with take on a CFO role with their clients, allowing the client to assume the role of the CEO and ultimately be in charge. This approach reinforces the idea that the advisor is working for the client and that the client is always in control.

The Need for Belonging

The third basic need is for acceptance and connection to other people. This need is related to Maslow's social need. Research shows that the groups we belong to play a vital role in our self-concept.[7] Our family, our friends, our church, and our ethnic groups are important to us and play an important role in our self-concept and our happiness. Therefore, we make the groups to which we belong a priority and look to them for support.

This need is relevant for a number of reasons. First, a sense of connection and belonging is at the heart of relationship-based marketing. The key to reaching the relationship level of branding and creating true loyalty is tapping into clients' need for belonging. Second, for many people, one of the main motivations for investing is to create security and opportunity for their family. Lastly, humans naturally categorize themselves into in-groups, meaning the groups to which they belong, and out-groups, meaning all other groups. There is a natural in-group bias through which people favor the groups to which they belong.[8] Even with arbitrarily created groups, multiple demonstrations have shown that people see themselves as more similar to, evaluate more highly, and reward more generously members of the groups to which they belong as compared to other groups.

This effect underscores the importance of looking for prospects within your own membership groups. As discussed in Chapter 4, ethnic groups to which you belong and industries to which you are connected make for good niches in part because prospects perceive you as part of their in-group. It also validates the tried-and-true practice of belonging to community groups as a prospecting tool. This is certainly effective for making contacts, but all things being equal, people are more likely to choose an advisor from a group to which they belong than someone who is not apparently affiliated with them.

The Need for Meaningfulness

The human is the only animal that is aware of its own mortality. Because we know that our time on earth is limited, we seek out ways to create things of significance and permanence that will endure. This basic need for meaningfulness is related to Maslow's notion of self-actualization.

A field of research related to this need for meaningfulness that is gaining much support is called terror management theory.[9] This research has shown that when people are presented with evidence of their own mortality, they cope, in part, by seeking out opportunities to create a sense of permanence, such as having children, seeking fame, believing in an afterlife, and creating other enduring legacies. Creating a legacy of wealth can sometimes be a means of creating a sense of permanence. It is very appealing to HNW individuals (and the not so HNW) to create a trust or endowment that will last "forever." People also seek out ways to have their money make a social or charitable impact that will endure. Nonprofits have effectively appealed to the desire for meaningfulness by granting naming rights or other permanent recognition for giving. Beyond tax advantages, seeking meaningfulness and an awareness of mortality can be a big factor in your clients' desire for trusts, endowments, estate planning, and philanthropy.

The first step of the decision-making process is recognizing a need, but as we have discussed, these needs can run deep. Clearly, a good financial advisor can assess the financial problems of her clients and create an effective financial plan to address these issues. However, those advisors who are the most effective at turning prospects into clients and creating long-term relationships are the ones who dig deeper and understand the core psychological needs that are driving the stated or easily observed need. In Chapter 9, we suggest creating a question protocol to help you discover what is truly motivating your clients and prospects.

INFORMATION SEARCH

When investors determine that they have a need that a financial advisor can help them satisfy, the next step in the decision-making process is to search for information. When the decision to invest, find an advisor, or change an advisor has been made, people will look for information on how to find the "right" person. This information search process occurs in two ways. First, people search their own memory for ways to satisfy their needs. This is called internal search. Second, they search externally for additional information, such as asking friends or searching the Internet.

The most important element to emerge from the information search process is a *consideration set*. A consideration set is a mental short list of ways to satisfy your need. In this case, the consideration is a short list of potential advisors. The consideration set is of the utmost importance because research consistently shows that options that are in the initial consideration set are overwhelmingly more likely to be ultimately chosen than options that are not. Thus, it is vital that you build awareness and are being recommended by your clients. This is where high levels of awareness through marketing communications, community involvement, good branding, and clients who consistently refer you pay dividends.

Information can be attained from a variety of sources, such as advertising, the Yellow Pages, and the Internet. However, information obtained from friends, family, and trusted centers of influence is by far the most influential. People are especially likely to rely on referrals and recommendations from others when their motivation is high and their knowledge is low, which is often the case when choosing a financial advisor.[10] Our research shows unequivocally that referrals drive the majority of business for financial advisors. Referrals were listed as the number one source of new business by a factor of more than three to one over the second and third most common sources, which were personal contacts and seminars. Additionally, our research shows that nearly 60 percent of all business is acquired directly through referrals from existing clients. Many advisors, especially more established ones, report that 100 percent of their new business comes from referrals. The dominance of referrals in client acquisition and within the decision-making process of clients underscores the importance of client relationship management. We discuss further how to cultivate and leverage these relationships in Chapter 7 and Chapter 9.

When making an important decision, current clients go through a decision-making process similar to that of prospects, with one important difference: their information search is dominated by their financial advisor. In a recent Abt SRBI survey of investors, 51 percent of investors stated that their advisor is their main source of investment information, and 48 percent listed their advisor as their most important source.[11] The Internet and friends/family were the second and third most cited sources. Advisors in our survey listed annual review meetings and proactive communication, such as phone calls, as the top ways in which their clients receive investment information from them. These data underscore the importance of proactively communicating investment information to clients. As we will discuss later in this chapter, an important driver of satisfaction among clients is the degree of proactive communication from a client's advisor.

EVALUATION OF ALTERNATIVES

Once a consideration set has been created, the client's next step is to evaluate the alternatives. A key distinction in this phase is the client's level of engagement. Highly engaged decision makers are more likely to make systematic and rational decisions in which they consider the pros and cons and weigh each one based on their own subjective estimate of its importance. In order to make a systematic evaluation, decision makers must possess three elements: *motivation, ability,* and *opportunity.*[12] If a decision maker lacks one or more of these elements, he must rely on a less rational approach, which we discuss later in this section.

Motivation is influenced by the salience of needs and goals, personal relevance, consistency with values, costs, and perceived risk. While one would think that everyone should be motivated when thinking about investing and financial planning, we all know that many people simply are not. A recent EBRI report[13] shows that 36 percent of workers have not saved for retirement at all. Additionally, the same report shows that less than half of workers have even casually tried to calculate how much money they will need for retirement. On the positive side, the data suggest that calculating these numbers can significantly influence motivation. Of those who performed a retirement savings calculation, nearly half changed their planning and nearly two-thirds started saving more.

Ability refers to intelligence, knowledge, experience, and education. As we will discuss in Chapter 6, the average level of financial literacy is quite low. The Abt SRBI report referred to earlier showed that 64 percent of investors rarely, very rarely, or never read prospectuses. While this statistic certainly is influenced by low motivation, the number one reason reported for not reading prospectuses was that they are too difficult to understand.

Opportunity is relatively straightforward. People need to have the time and information to make an informed decision. "I just don't have time" is clearly a big problem that is difficult to overcome. This is especially true for high-net-worth clients, who are extremely busy doing what it is that makes them high net worth. The data in our study suggest that patience and persistence on the part of the advisor are critical in getting prospects and clients to make a decision. As we will discuss in the next chapter, it is effective to frame decisions over longer periods of time.

Assuming that a prospect or client has all three of the elements needed to make a systematic decision about getting or changing an advisor, what are the critical items that are factored into the decision? We critically reviewed multiple investor studies and surveys, as well as the views of the more than 800 advisors in our study. These items emerge across multiple sources as driving clients' choice of advisor:

- Trust
- Investment performance
- Deep understanding of individual needs/situation
- Expertise/knowledge of the advisor
- Quality service
- Clear articulation of fees
- Partnering/education/client control

While all of these elements are important, which ones really can differentiate you from your competition? It is highly unlikely that you would be in the consideration set if your prospects did not assume that you were trustworthy and could deliver solid investment performance. While trust seems to top the list on many of the surveys, performance is not the dominant factor that many would assume it to be. In a recent study published by colleagues of ours at the Wharton School,[14] only 10 percent of investors named investment performance as the most important factor in choosing a financial advisor. Performance was fifth on the list, behind trust (69 percent), understanding of needs (20 percent), communication (16 percent), and low fees (12 percent).

While you certainly should not ignore trust and performance, these factors will not differentiate you from your competition. For instance, safety is often cited as a prime consideration when choosing an airline. However, while safety is very important, domestic airlines are all virtually tied for first, and so safety really doesn't factor into consumers' final decisions to fly one carrier rather than another.

As we discussed in Chapter 4, the factors listed here are important and provide you with the opportunity to differentiate yourself on one, while trying to achieve parity on the others.

What happens when a decision maker lacks motivation, ability, or opportunity? That person is not able to make a systematic assessment of the critical factors, so she must rely on another strategy. These decision makers are likely to use a *heuristic*. A heuristic is a choice tactic, or rule of thumb, that is used to make a quick decision when one lacks motivation, ability, or opportunity. Consumers use heuristics for all types of day-to-day decisions. For instance, many people lack the expertise to make an informed choice from a wine list, so they use a price-quality heuristic. That is, they use price as a guideline or rule of thumb to infer the quality of the wine.

While we will discuss heuristics in more depth in Chapter 6, there are a number of heuristics that can influence the decision to choose a particular advisor. For instance, an "expert recommended" heuristic influences many choices we make when we lack information. This is a powerful influence in choosing professional services. Referrals from trusted advisors or centers of influence like lawyers and accountants are often heeded without any additional consideration. Another powerful rule of thumb is the normative heuristic, which suggests that if everybody is doing something, it must be good. Advertising regularly seeks to harness this by making claims such as "the number-one-selling brand" or "ten million people can't be wrong." This is another advantage of a niche strategy, because when you advise several people within a niche, you can become the normative or default choice for that group.

Sometimes it is easy to tell whether someone is making a systematic or a heuristic evaluation. Other times, it is not. It is sound marketing practice to provide reasons to choose your brand that have appeal across both systematic and heuristic assessments. You should certainly have clear and easily articulated evidence to support your qualifications on the critical decision factors listed earlier. Additionally, your communication should be especially cogent on your key points of differentiation. However, you should also provide heuristic cues such as accreditations and affiliations to communicate expertise, references to clients that prospects know to position yourself as the normative choice, and professionally printed materials that spell out your services and fees to imply openness and trust.

THE PURCHASE DECISION

Getting the client to actually "pull the trigger" and make a decision is clearly the most difficult step. As we stated before, persistence and patience are key elements. The advisors in our study indicate that following up on prospects is the critical element in turning them into clients. Simply put, many advisors give up too soon. Our data show that it takes more than six months, on average, to turn a prospect into a client. A prospect is unlikely to become a client during your first interaction. Effective advisors agree that the purpose of the first meeting is not to close the sale; rather, the purpose is to get the second meeting. You must adjust your expectations and realize that decision making is, in fact, a process.

Additionally, getting a small piece of a prospect's business can open the door for bigger things in the future. While you may want to get all of a client's business right away, that is a difficult decision for most prospects to make. It is easier for prospects to dip their toe in the water, so to speak, than to turn over tens of thousands or even millions of dollars all at once. Moreover, research suggests that you are more likely to ultimately get a large dollar wallet share by starting out small than by trying to get it all at once. Dating back to 1966,[15] a large body of research on the foot-in-the-door technique shows that influencers who get targets to comply with a small request are much more likely to get them to comply with a larger request later.

The most important reason that the foot-in-the-door technique works is that it creates psychological momentum and commitment. Once a prospect commits to the course of action of investing with you, even with a trivial amount, increasing that commitment becomes much easier as time goes on. This is a tried-and-true technique that top salespeople have used forever and that is part of the rationale behind "free" samples. Furthermore, managing even a small amount gives you the opportunity to prove your competence and build trust. Many times an incremental approach such as this will deliver a long-term payoff.

Seth Godin, in his book *Permission Marketing: Turning Strangers into Friends and Friends into Customers,*[16] gives another take on the incremental approach to closing. Permission marketing is based on anticipated, personal, and increasingly relevant messages. The premise is that if strangers are to ultimately become loyal customers, they must go though a long-term relationship-building process (see Figure 5.4). Moreover, this process must begin before the client invests his first dollar. As Godin states, "It's silly to ask strangers to become customers without spending time

Figure 5.4 The Permission Marketing Ladder

Loyalty

↑

Customer

↑

Relationship

↑

Stranger

to teach them, to gain their trust, and to have a mutually beneficial dialogue instead of a narcissistic monologue." You must develop the relationship to the point where the prospect gives you permission to sell.

The bottom line is that the purchase or investment decision is not made in an instant. It is a process that you can influence. This requires patience, persistence, and a long-term perspective. While everyone hopes for a client who will immediately transfer millions of dollars at the first meeting, the reality is that "A" clients are more likely to be created through long-term relationship building and incremental increases in assets under management. Of course, strong referrals can accelerate that process.

POSTDECISION PROCESSES

Perhaps the most critical, but most ignored, part of the decision-making process occurs after the actual purchase or investment decision has been made. This is the point at which clients assess the value of the outcome. It is at this stage that satisfaction, retention, loyalty, and ultimately referrals are the focus. In this section, we will discuss what drives satisfaction and how advisors can manage expectations to engender greater levels of satisfaction and loyalty.

One would think that good performance and high quality would be the primary drivers of satisfaction. In reality, there is a very low correlation between objective performance or quality and satisfaction. When people make assessments of satisfaction (or dissatisfaction), research shows that the key driver is the client's subjective expectations. Specifically, satisfaction or dissatisfaction occurs when there is a discrepancy, either positive or negative, between subjective expectations and perceived performance. This process is called *disconfirmation*,[17] and it has dominated the way thoughtful and experienced marketers understand satisfaction.

The critical element of the disconfirmation paradigm suggests that people are always comparing outcomes to expectations. For example, we would intuitively expect a meal at a five-star restaurant to produce higher levels of satisfaction than lunch at a local diner. However, while the meal at the fancy restaurant may objectively be much better than a tuna melt at the local diner, it must measure up to the lofty expectations that come with it. If the food is good but not great and the service is a bit snooty, our expectations will not be met and we will be left with low levels of satisfaction. In contrast, we are likely to have modest expectations when we stop into a small diner for a cheap lunch. If the food is enjoyable and the service is friendly, our expectations will be exceeded, leading to higher levels of satisfaction. In this example, the diner produces higher levels of satisfaction and probably more loyalty than the fancy expensive restaurant, despite the fact the food at the fancy place is objectively of higher quality.

The mantra that is attached to the disconfirmation approach is to never overpromise, but consistently and modestly overdeliver. A good example of this in practice is the way in which Amazon.com communicates its delivery times. When a customer chooses regular ground transportation, the Web site gives an estimated delivery time of seven to nine days. In fact, the average delivery time is much quicker, but communicating the actual average delivery time would ensure that half of the recipients would be disappointed by a subjectively "late" delivery. Keep in mind that overdelivering does not mean sandbagging. This is why we specifically say modestly overdeliver. In contrast, good advisors set realistic expectations that can consistently and modestly be exceeded.

This understanding of satisfaction indicates that managing expectations is just as important as your actual performance. Of course you need to provide good service and strong investment performance. However, if your good work is to produce satisfaction, it must outperform your client's expectations. You must assess how your clients set their expectations. How quickly do they expect you to return calls? How much time do they expect to spend with you on a regular basis? How do they expect to be informed about fees and commissions? What are their comparison points for assessing investment performance? These are all expectations that you should be actively managing. If you do not do so, there is no telling how realistically your clients will set their expectations.

Furthermore, expectations are something that you should assess and begin to manage *before* a person becomes your client. If a prospect has unrealistic expectations for service and performance that you are unlikely to be able to meet, you are better off not having her as a client. (See Chapter 7 for computing client value and "firing" unprofitable customers.) Likewise, it is a mistake to overpromise to a client just to close a sale. People rarely adjust their expectations downward. Realistically, these clients are doomed to be dissatisfied, and they probably will not last long. If they do stick around, they certainly will not recommend you.

In addition, it is important that referrals do not become a source of unrealistic expectations. If those who spread word of mouth about you are promising something that you can't deliver, they may be setting those prospective clients up for dissatisfaction as well. Making sure that your clients are talking to the right prospective clients and saying the right things is as important as getting the referral in the first place. Failure to assess and manage expectations is one of the biggest mistakes that advisors make when trying to build their client list. Taking on a client who is not a good match with your strengths and whose expectations are too high is a bad long-run strategy.

Beyond expectations, it is important to recognize the factors that investors identify as being critical to their satisfaction and retention. As in choosing an advisor, investors want good financial performance, individualized understanding of their needs, and responsive service. However, two critical elements that are most likely to produce dissatisfaction and damage retention are poor communication and poor articulation of fees. In one recent study,[18] the most common reason given for switching advisors was dissatisfaction with advisors' maintenance of proactive communication. According to a Cogent Research study,[19] the biggest performance gap contributing to dissatisfaction is in the explanation of fees and costs associated with investments. It should be noted that in both of these studies, communication and fee articulation emerge as more important drivers of satisfaction than good investment performance.

Satisfaction is clearly the key to creating loyal clients who will ultimately be a source of referrals. Only through consistently satisfying your clients will those clients become the loyal ambassadors who help build your business for the long term.

CONCLUSIONS

Clients' decisions to choose an advisor, switch advisors, or significantly change their level of assets under management are driven by multiple factors. Advisors need to understand the stages in client decision making and how this process can influence clients at critical junctures. Your business begins and ends with clients, so understanding them is vital. The themes that emerge from this chapter, such as relationship building, a long-term approach, proactive communication, and managing expectations, are echoed throughout our study of effective advisors and throughout the other chapters of this book.

NOTES

1. Abraham H. Maslow, *Motivation and Personality*, 2nd ed. (New York: Harper & Row, 1970).
2. Abraham Tesser, "Self-Esteem," in Abraham Tesser and Norbert Schwartz (eds.), *Blackwell Handbook*

of Social Psychology: Intraindividual Process (Malden, Mass.: Blackwell Publishers, 2001), pp. 479–498.

3. Shelly E. Taylor and Jonathon D. Brown, "Illusions and Well-Being: A Social Psychological Perspective on Mental Health," *Psychological Bulletin* 103 (1988), 193–210.

4. S. J. Spencer, R. A. Josephs, and C. M. Steele, "Low Self-Esteem: The Uphill Struggle for Self-Integrity," in R. F. Baumeister (ed.), *Self-Esteem and the Puzzle of Low Self-Regard* (New York: Wiley, 1993).

5. Russell W. Belk, "Possessions and the Extended Self," *Journal of Consumer Research*, September 1988, pp. 139–168.

6. S. E. Taylor and L. G. Aspinwall, "Mediating and Moderating Processes in Psychosocial Stress: Appraisal, Coping, Resistance and Vulnerability," in H. B. Kaplan (ed.), *Psychosocial Stress: Perspectives on Structure, Theory, Life-Course, and Methods* (San Diego, Calif.: Academic Press, 1996), pp. 71–110.

7. H. Tajfel, "Social Psychology of Intergroup Attitudes," *Annual Review of Psychology* 33 (1982), 1–39.

8. H. Tajfel and J. C. Turner, "The Social Identity Theory of Intergroup Behavior," in S. Worshel and W. G. Austin (eds.), *Psychology of Intergroup Relations*, 2nd ed. (Chicago: Nelson-Hall, 1986), pp. 7–24.

9. S. Solomon, J. Greenberg, and T. Pyszczynski, "A Terror Management Theory of Social Behavior: The Psychological Functions of Self-Esteem and Cultural Worldviews," *Advances in Experimental Social Psychology* 24 (1991), 93–159.

10. David F. Midgley, "Patterns of Interpersonal Information Seeking for the Purchase of a Symbolic Product," *Journal of Marketing Research*, February 1983, pp. 74–83.

11. Abt SRBI, *Mandatory Disclosure Documents Telephone Survey*, submitted to the Securities and Exchange Commission Office of Investor Education and Advocacy, July 30, 2008.

12. Wayne D. Hoyer and Deborah J. MacInnis, *Consumer Behavior* (Boston: Houghton Mifflin, 2006).

13. Employee Benefit Research Institute, *2008 Retirement Confidence Survey*, EBRI Issue Brief 316, April 2008.

14. Knowledge@Wharton and State Street Global Advisors, *Bridging the Trust Divide: The Financial Advisor-Client Relationship*, Special Report, 2008.

15. J. L. Freedman and S. C. Fraser, "Compliance without Pressure: The Foot-in-the-Door Technique," *Journal of Personality and Social Psychology* 4 (1966), 195–202.

16. Seth Godin, *Permission Marketing: Turning Strangers into Friends and Friends into Customers* (New York: Simon & Schuster, 1999).

17. Richard L. Oliver, "A Cognitive Model of the Antecedents and Consequences of Satisfaction Decisions," *Journal of Marketing Research*, November 1980, pp. 460–469.

18. 2007 Phoenix Wealth Survey.

19. Barclay's Global Investors, *Measuring Affluent and HNW Investor Expectations of the Investment and Financial Community*, report prepared by Cogent Research for iShares, March 2008.

CHAPTER 6

INVESTOR PSYCHOLOGY AND BIASES

L ogically, we expect people to be "maximizers." That is, we expect purely rational decision makers to analyze the available information and make a decision that maximizes their potential for return. However, anyone who has been involved in financial planning for any length of time knows that clients do not always make decisions that are in their own best interests. Clients sometimes insist on sabotaging themselves despite your best advice. Investors routinely stick with suboptimal allocations, let emotions influence their decisions, throw good money after bad into losing strategies, chase past momentum, and put off doing the necessary routine maintenance of their retirement plans.

Standard economic models assume efficient markets and rational investors, but we all know that markets are not always efficient and investors certainly are not always rational. However, does this mean that they are irrational? Crazy? Stupid? Not exactly. All investors are human and thus have shortcomings and biases in their thought and

decision-making processes. So, we are not so much irrational as systematically biased. In his bestselling book *Predictably Irrational*, Dan Ariely[1] describes the many ways in
which our cognitive systems and individual psychology lead
us to less than optimal, and sometimes just plain strange,
behavior. Researchers in psychology, marketing, finance,
and economics have all studied these biases intensely. Out of
this multidisciplinary research, a new field called behavioral
economics has emerged to study exactly how this systematic
bias affects investors and the broader markets.

In the following pages, we will highlight some of the most
important findings and insights from all of this research.
Among other things, we will discuss how the framing of
information, faulty decision-making strategies, perceptions
of risk, and emotions can produce undesirable outcomes for
investors. The goal is not only to help you understand why
your clients do some of the things they do, but also to give
you some strategies for dealing with this and to help you
help them make better decisions.

CONTEXT AND COMPLEXITY

The landscape of investing has become increasingly complex. One reason is the continuous availability of information. We are constantly besieged with financial information.
Twenty-four-hour cable networks like CNBC, Bloomberg,
and CNN, along with thousands of Internet sites, provide
up-to-the-second financial news and analysis. This glut of
information can be intoxicating for some investors, but is it
good for them? As we will discuss later in this chapter, looking at the daily changes of an investment or portfolio causes

investors to unduly focus on the short term. This can often have the negative effect of encouraging investors to lose focus on a long-term strategy and can lead them to make multiple rash decisions. Some have dubbed the connection between the increased availability of financial information and increased trading the "CNBC effect."

Furthermore, the uncertain economics of the twenty-first century has complicated matters further, but there may be a silver lining. While the volatile market creates anxiety among clients and may make your job harder, it also can make you, the financial advisor, more valuable. In the *Wall Street Journal*, Wharton professor and finance legend Jeremy Siegel addressed the financial turmoil of 2008, saying, "In fact the current crisis could well lead to an increase in the demand for financial services, as the world grapples with the need for new financial instruments, new risk management techniques, and the increasing complexity of the financial world."[2]

Other changes in the economic landscape have further complicated things for investors. For instance, the broad move from defined-benefit to defined-contribution plans has shifted responsibility for retirement planning to investors and created a new level of uncertainty. As we discussed in Chapter 3, the demographic trends in the United States have created a huge market for retirement planning, as individuals need help navigating these uncertain waters. Additionally, this shift to defined-contribution plans, along with the wave of retiring baby boomers, has put millions of people in a wealth-management role. Retiring with large sums of money, combined with the global emerging wealth trends, has indeed thrust many individuals into complex money-management situations that require skilled advice.

Further adding to the complexity is that the sheer number of ways to invest has exploded over the last several years. The number of mutual funds alone has grown exponentially, and investment options continue to expand. However, *increased choice* has a peculiar effect on investors, simultaneously both attracting and repelling them. When we consider the notion of "choice," we tend to think of it as purely a good thing. Especially in the United States, we live in a culture that values choice. Also, there is plenty of research demonstrating that individuals are happier when they perceive that they have a choice. Making choices is often associated with a sense of personal autonomy, control over one's life, and a feeling of empowerment. Individuals are often more satisfied overall when they can make choices, even if those choices are trivial.[3] Despite all these positive outcomes associated with more choice, however, there can also be a downside associated with such freedoms.

Consider a Columbia University study[4] looking at the issue of choice. A sample table was set up in a grocery store offering either 24 or 6 different jams to taste. When the table offered a wide variety of jams to sample, 60 percent of shoppers stopped and tried at least one jam. When six jams were offered, only 40 percent of shoppers stopped. Clearly, a wider selection led to increased interest among shoppers. However, only 3 percent of the shoppers who sampled from the large array actually purchased a jar of jam. In contrast, 30 percent of those who sampled from the smaller array made a purchase. While a large choice set is attractive to consumers, it has the ironic effect of making the actual choice more difficult, consequently reducing the likelihood of action.

The Columbia researchers followed up this experiment by letting consumers sample chocolates from either a large (30) or small (6) array of choices and rate their favorite. Probabilistically, we would expect that a favorite chosen from a large set would be more highly rated than one chosen from a small set because you would be more likely to find one that closely matches individual tastes. In contrast, the favorites chosen from the small choice set were rated significantly higher than those chosen from the large set. Additionally, participants in the study were given a choice between taking their favorite chocolate or $5 as a reward for completing the experiment. In the large choice set condition, only 12 percent of participants chose to take the chocolate, while nearly 50 percent of participants in the small choice set condition did. These findings suggest that not only do smaller choice sets make decisions easier and increase sales, but more limited choice sets also, paradoxically, increase satisfaction by making the decision easier. We tend to think that the process of deciding or buying is separate from an individual's satisfaction with the actual item purchases, such as the jam or the chocolate in these studies. However, these results suggest that the process of deciding which items to buy has a direct influence on how satisfied we are with those items.

Extending these findings to investing, a separate follow-up study analyzed company retirement plans managed by Vanguard.[5] Of course, HR directors and employees alike are attracted to plans that offer lots of choices. However, the researchers found that an abundance of choices actually had a detrimental effect on plan participation. There was a clear negative correlation between the number of investment choices available and the enrollment of employees in the plan. In fact, for every 10 additional investment choices, there was a 2 percent reduction in employee participation. These results are attributed to the difficulty that consumers have in choosing how to make their initial investments. Strangely, many prefer not to choose at all because the choices are difficult, despite an initial preference for more choice. This dilemma has been characterized as the *paradox of choice*.[6] People want lots of choices, but increased choice options can ultimately reduce the odds of making a choice. Moreover, having too many options in the choice set can lower the resulting satisfaction with the chosen alternative even when a choice is made.

So what does the paradox of choice mean to a financial advisor? It means that you have to be very careful about the amount of choice you present to investors and when you do it. When you are trying to attract a client, a large choice set is an advantage. Clients will want lots of options and flexibility, and having this will be seen as an advantage. However, you clearly want to limit the choice set when it comes time for the client to actually make a decision. This is not to say that you cannot "open up the book" and add more options later, but a very well chosen and finite array of options will increase the likelihood of your clients actually making a choice. Thus, you must be selective in the options you reveal to your clients and judicious in your timing. This also suggests that in situations where you are not in control of the complete choice set—for example, when you are helping your clients make decisions about employee benefit options—you will nonetheless want to help them to reduce the number of options to choose from so that they are more likely to make appropriate decisions.

FINANCIAL LITERACY

Investors are navigating a complex world with an overabundance of choices. The next logical question becomes: how much do investors really know? Sadly, on average, they do not know enough. Survey after survey reveals that the average investor possesses a very low level of *financial literacy*. For instance, an Opinion Research Corporation study[7] revealed that 83 percent of investors failed a test of basic financial knowledge and fundamental concepts. Some key findings from the study:

• Only 66 percent of investors correctly identified stocks (as opposed to bonds, CDs, and savings accounts) as having the highest return over the last 25 years.
• A full 59 percent did not understand that bond prices tend to fall as interest rates rise.
• Only 8 percent understood that no federal agency insures against investment fraud.
• A full 61 percent did not know that a no-load mutual fund involves no commission.
• Only 57 percent could define a prospectus correctly.

Other studies show similarly low levels of financial literacy. A John Hancock survey[8] found that 40 percent of respondents believed that money market funds contain stocks. The same study revealed that the average investor believes that company stock is less risky than a mutual fund. Multiple surveys show that most investors have no idea what an annuity is and do not understand its advantages and disadvantages.

This is not to say that there are not some very well-educated investors out there or that you do not have some clients who are very well informed. It is clear, however, that the average investor lacks much of the basic knowledge necessary to make informed financial choices. Even somewhat informed investors may know less than they think they know.

Despite their generally low levels of financial literacy, investors' confidence in their own financial savvy tends to be high. Studies reveal a clear inconsistency between investors' knowledge and their confidence. For instance, a Cogent Research study[9] showed that while nearly 90 percent of investors claimed to fully understand the level of risk in their portfolio, only about 60 percent said that they could confidently communicate the purpose of each investment. Many other studies reveal similarly high levels of *overconfidence*.

Ironically, this widespread overconfidence is fueled by the wide availability of financial information. There is a phenomenon called the *illusion of knowledge* that shows that as people get additional information, even if that information is ambiguous or irrelevant, they become more confident in their decisions. That is, the more people watch CNBC, the more likely they are to think that they know quite a bit about investing. However, their accuracy is not, in fact, significantly improved with the additional information. Perhaps less surprising is that many studies, across a variety of situations, show a very low correlation between confidence and accuracy.

Overconfidence has been linked to high levels of churn in portfolios and overall lower returns. It has a significant correlation with high trade frequency, especially among men. That is, men are more likely to be overconfident and, as a result, engage in more frequent trades. In fact, the average turnover rate of common stocks for men is 1.5 times that for women. Both men and women reduce their net returns through trading, but men reduce their returns by about 1 percent more than women do. The effect is even stronger when comparing single men with single women.[10] Another study analyzing thousands of online brokerage accounts showed that the 20 percent of people who traded the most underperformed the market by 10 percent.[11] These findings combine to suggest that overconfidence can lead to rash decisions and churn that ultimately produce lower returns.

HEURISTICS

As we discussed in Chapter 5, people need motivation, ability, and opportunity in order to make rational and systematic decisions. When people lack one or more of these elements, they rely on heuristics. A heuristic is a resource-saving choice tactic, or, more simply, a rule of thumb. If we are unmotivated, lack the ability or knowledge (as many investors do), or just do not have time, we will employ one of these choice tactics. For instance, the *normative heuristic* is a rule of thumb that says that if everyone is doing something, it must be good. Advertisements claiming that something is "the number-one-selling brand" are trying to appeal to this heuristic by implying that "millions of people can't be wrong." While this might work fine for choosing a laundry detergent, the stakes are much higher when making financial decisions. Investors often rely too much on tactics like the normative heuristic to make decisions in the absence of a deeper analysis.

The *availability heuristic* is an extremely common choice tactic that often influences investment decisions. The availability heuristic is the judgment of the likelihood of something based on how quickly we can call examples to mind.[12] For example, people routinely overestimate violent crime rates because examples of crimes are so readily available in memory. A recent and vivid news story can overwhelm the actual statistical base rates. In fact, most of us often have no knowledge of the statistical base rates for things like violent crime, but it is easy to recite stories that we've heard on the news about a violent occurrence. Thus, the available example is weighted more heavily in our judgments.

Availability can bias clients to overinvest in things with which they are very familiar. For example, roughly 5 million Americans have over 60 percent of their retirement savings in their own company's stock and generally view their company's stock as being safer than a diversified portfolio.[13] It is hard to make an argument that *any* single stock is better than a diversified portfolio, but familiarity often trumps logic. The vividness and availability of information on our own company is more compelling and more easily understood than the nebulous information about indexes and broader markets. Other research has described a similar "all that glitters" effect,[14] showing that investors tend to be net buyers of attention-grabbing stocks that are mentioned often in the media. The vast majority of investors have difficulty sorting through the thousands of individual stocks that they could buy, so they rely on the increased availability of information on particular stocks.

A related heuristic, *representativeness*, occurs when the evaluation of an item or event is affected by the resemblance of that item or event to a similar predecessor.[15] That is, does something match up to our stereotype? Like availability, representativeness is marked by an underuse of base rate or statistical information. For example, imagine that there is a room with 100 people in it. In that room, 70 of the people are farmers and 30 are lawyers. If I choose one person at random and describe her as articulate, argumentative, and intelligent, would you guess that she is a farmer or a lawyer? The vast majority of people guess lawyer when they are given this problem. They rely on their stereotype of a lawyer. However, the base rate for the population in the room indicates that there is a much better chance (70 percent) that she is a farmer. Even though it is clear that the odds are against it, people guess lawyer because the description is representative of what we expect a lawyer to be like.

We use heuristics all the time because they provide us with quick ways of making satisfactory judgments. Representativeness bias effectively says that if it quacks and waddles, it is a duck. Most of the time, this type of quick judgment allows us to skip a more detailed analysis and produce an answer that is good enough. Who cares if it is a duck or a goose? However, the outcome can be costly when we over-apply heuristics in situations with higher stakes than ducks versus geese.

For example, people are always looking for the next Google, the next fast-growing emerging market, or the next dot-com sector. That is natural, but the problem is that it is easier for an investment to *look* like a winner than to actually *be* a winner. In short, heuristics can lead investors to *chase momentum*. For instance, research on mutual funds shows that strong past performance leads to an increased inflow of assets into a particular fund.[16] Advisors know that the funds with eye-popping returns over the past year sell themselves.

We all preach that past performance does not guarantee future returns, but availability and representativeness lead investors to believe otherwise.

Again, it is really the misapplication and overapplication of heuristics that is the problem. For instance, no one would argue that diversification is a bad thing. However, investors hear so much about diversification that they pursue it in ways that may be irrational. We have all seen clients who own several different mutual funds in the name of diversification, but these funds all own the same underlying stocks, giving the client no real additional diversification. This *diversification heuristic* has a particularly large impact when there is a predetermined set of investments available, as in many 401(k) plans. A typical response to a choice of funds within a retirement plan is to invest evenly across all of the choices, putting a small portion of money into each of the funds.[17] Not only is this a poor application of an otherwise sound principal of investing, but it can produce dramatically different allocations depending on the funds contained in the plan.

This was demonstrated in an experiment in which people were asked to allocate money across a set of five mutual funds.[18] One group was given a set of four fixed-income funds and one stock fund to choose from. The resulting allocations had an average equity share of 43 percent. Another group was given a set of four stock funds and one fixed-income fund. This group had an average equity share of 68 percent. As is evident, the choice set and propensity to diversify led to two very different resulting allocations. Analysis of actual retirement plans indicates that the set of available investment choices affects allocations in the same manner. Plans with more equity funds tended to have allocations that were more heavily weighted toward stocks. This heuristic leads to a misperception that diversification has been achieved simply by spreading money across a set of alternatives. Thus, heuristics can get people into trouble when they are combined with a context, frame, or choice set that makes the application of these heuristics problematic.

PSYCHOLOGICAL INERTIA

Probably the most consistent complaint that we hear from financial advisors is that they can't get their clients to make a decision. They complain that their clients will often understand what is the best thing to do, but just can't seem to pull the trigger. Clients know that they need to reallocate their portfolio, invest more aggressively, or update their estate plan, but they keep putting it off. Sometimes, even getting clients to set up a meeting or return a call can be a challenge. Other times, clients will insist on following through with a losing strategy, like overinvesting in a certain sector or company stock. One powerful force behind these problems is *psychological inertia*.

Psychological inertia is analogous to physical inertia. We know from physics that bodies that are in motion tend to stay in motion, while bodies that are at rest tend to stay at rest. A similar principle applies in psychology. When we are engaged in a course of action or invested in a particular image of ourselves, the tendency is to remain consistently committed to that course or image. Likewise, when we are stagnant or inactive, it requires a great deal of psychological energy to compel us into action. That is, we tend to stay at psychological rest. Two common examples of inertia-based effects are the *status quo bias* and the *sunk cost effect*.

The status quo bias is the tendency for us to stick with our current situation or choices. Doing nothing by sticking with what we have now is often easier than mustering the psychological energy needed to overcome inertia. Magazines and other services often take advantage of this bias by giving away "free" subscriptions that must be canceled or they automatically become paid subscriptions. The promise that "you can cancel anytime" is made with the knowledge that the status quo bias is on the side of the company. This same type of inaction can have a detrimental effect for investors. An analysis of TIAA-CREF participants showed that the median number of reallocations in a lifetime was zero.[19] This study and several others show that initial investment allocations are critically important because they have enduring impact. Moreover, status quo bias fuels the client procrastination that can be so frustrating to FAs.

The sunk cost effect describes not only our reluctance to realize our own losses, but also the tendency to follow those losses with additional investment. In other words, sometimes investors throw good money after bad. The sunk cost effect can be explained in part by our desire to avoid realizing losses, which we will discuss in detail in the next section, on loss aversion. However, personal attachment or felt responsibility also has a strong effect. In one classic study, participants played the role of managers who were to decide whether to invest R&D money in an underperforming business unit or spend it elsewhere in the company. Half of the participants were told that they had previously made an unprofitable investment in that unit, and the other half were told that another manager had made that decision. Results showed that the managers who felt responsible for the previous investment made significantly higher additional R&D

investments.[20] Thus, the psychological commitment to a previous action, even when it was a losing strategy, increased the likelihood of repeating that action. Similar results have been found in dozens of other studies across a wide range of real-life and experimental situations.

Inertia-based effects, like the ones discussed here, rest on a foundation of two highly related constructs: *anticipated regret* and *normality bias*. To explain, consider these two clients:

- Mr. Davis owns stock in Company A. During the past year, he considered switching to stock in Company B, but he decided against it. He now finds out that he would have been better off by $10,000 if he had switched to Company B.
- Mr. Johnson owned stock in Company B. During the past year, he switched to stock in Company A. He now finds that he would have been better off by $10,000 if he had kept his stock in Company B.

Who feels worse, Mr. Davis or Mr. Johnson? This scenario, as well as many other examples and findings in this chapter, is based on research by Nobel laureate Daniel Kahneman and Amos Tversky.[21] When we present this problem to advisors, they agree, as did the subjects in the original study, that Mr. Johnson feels much worse. But why is this true? Whenever we make a decision (or decide to do nothing), we imagine how that decision could turn out. Naturally, we tend to look ahead and imagine ways in which things could go wrong. In other words, we anticipate how we could end up regretting our actions. For many decisions, this is enough to keep us from acting. We do not want to end up kicking ourselves and saying, "I should have just left well enough alone." Like Mr. Johnson in the scenario just given, we tend to feel worse about bad outcomes that stem from our actions rather than from inaction.

Anticipated regret tends to bias us toward inaction or whatever we view as our current default condition. For instance, advisors routinely report that clients are apprehensive about reallocating their portfolios. They get the feeling that "as soon as I move more money into stocks, the market will tank." However, are we more likely to regret action or inaction? As the name *normality bias* suggests, the default condition is a matter of perspective. Whether we are talking about action (the sunk cost effect) or inaction (the status quo bias), we tend to be biased toward what we perceive to be the default or normal thing. Therein lies the key to understanding and dealing with inertial effects. You must diagnose what the perceived default condition is and, if necessary, change it.

Consider how people buy automobile insurance in New Jersey and Pennsylvania. Both states have a so-called limited tort option. That is, you can pay a lower rate if you give up your right to sue for pain and suffering for injuries that fall under a certain threshold. In New Jersey, 80 percent of drivers choose the lower-priced limited tort option. In Pennsylvania, however, only 25 percent make the same choice, with 75 percent choosing the higher-priced full tort option.[22] Are New Jersey drivers that much more frugal? Probably not. The reason for the huge difference is that drivers in the two states have different perceived default conditions, or states of normality. In Pennsylvania, the higher-priced option is the default, and in order to select the lower-priced limited tort option, you must explicitly indicate that you are waiving your right to sue under certain conditions. It is just the opposite in New Jersey. The lower-priced option is the default, and you must take action to preserve your right to sue. While the "action" required to change the default condition in either case involves nothing more than checking a box and signing your name, the psychological inertia is much more difficult to overcome, as it biases drivers toward the default condition regardless of their true preference.

The insurance scenario is an example of the *opt-in versus opt-out* problem. Consider a new hire at a Fortune 500 company. The default condition is that this new employee is not a 401(k) participant and must fill out paperwork to enroll. This situation is typical and is called opt-in. While most people clearly understand the benefits of a 401(k), data show that rates of participation when opt-in is the default condition can be as low as 26 percent for new hires and 57 percent for employees after even three years.[23] However, companies with automatic enrollment, or an opt-out default, have 401(k) participation that is nearly 50 percent higher on average.[24] The benefits and logic of participating in the plan are the same under both the opt-in and the opt-out conditions. The only difference is the perceived default condition and the direction of the psychological inertia. Opt-out makes being enrolled the default condition and puts inertia on the side of the employee.

Similarly impressive results have been realized using a program called *Save More Tomorrow* (SMT).[25] This program is a contribution rate escalator in which retirement plan participants precommit to future increases in their savings rates tied to future pay increases. The typical advice given to participants is to increase savings now, which can be painful and requires the decision maker to overcome psychological inertia. With the

SMT program, procrastination is harnessed by asking people to commit today to increases that will happen automatically in the future. As we will discuss in more depth later in this chapter, inertia and anticipated regret are much more powerful in the near term than they are in the distant future. In addition, people tend to be myopic. That is, they are focused on today rather than tomorrow, and they think that they will be able to save more in the future, even though they deem it too painful to do now. Thus, people are much more inclined to agree to do something six months or a year down the road than they are to do it now. In one analysis, SMT increased contribution rates from 3.5 percent to 13.6 percent, nearly four times the previous savings rate, over 40 months.

Both automatic enrollment programs and SMT are ingenious because they harness inertia. They change the perceived default so that inertia is working for the investor instead of against her. Going back to the problem of getting clients to meet with you and make decisions, the most common thing that advisors do is call clients and try to set up a time to meet in the near future. In this situation, inertia is working against you because the client has to take action to set up the meeting (opt-in) and will probably have to alter her investment plan from what she has already been doing (change the status quo). This is working against the inertia. If, instead, you schedule a reallocation meeting six months in advance, the client can cancel, but doing so is much harder psychologically (it is opt-out). Here, the client must change the status quo to *not* meet with you and address her issues. Thus, a regularly scheduled meeting *becomes* the status quo because you have changed the perceived default.

In addition, just as everyone thinks that he will have more money to invest in the future, everyone thinks that his schedule will be freer in the future. Clients are more likely to agree to an appointment six months in advance, when the calendar is full of empty space, than a week in advance, when their calendar is full.[26] Inertia does not predetermine behavior, but it certainly biases us toward defaults. The key is to harness inertia by changing the perceived defaults.

HOW DO INVESTORS PERCEIVE LOSSES AND RISK?

It certainly comes as no surprise to find out that investors hate losses. However, losses are often a matter of perspective and are highly influenced by the framing of information. Consider this scenario:

- In addition to whatever you own, you have been given $1,000. You are now asked to choose between A and B.
  Choice A: A 50 percent chance of gaining $1,000
  Choice B: A sure gain of $500

Note that in this scenario, you have gained $1,000 immediately and you then have a chance to *gain* more. Probabilistically, Choice A and Choice B are equivalent. From a pure probability standpoint, the utility of Choice A is 0.5 × $1,000, which is worth $500. Choice B is evidently worth $500. However, the choices feel very different psychologically. In the original version of this study,[27] participants overwhelmingly picked Choice B, the sure thing. In many replications, including demonstrations we have conducted in our classes and executive education seminars, respondents have consistently shown a strong preference for the conservative, risk-averse choice. Now consider this scenario:

- In addition to whatever you own, you have been given $2,000. You are now asked to choose between A and B.
  Choice A: A 50 percent chance of losing $1,000
  Choice B: A sure loss of $500

Unlike the situation in the first scenario, you have immediately gained $2,000, but there is a chance of *losing* some of it. As in the first scenario, both choices are probabilistically equivalent, with a utility of -$500. In this scenario, however, participants consistently choose the riskier Choice A. Unlike in the previous scenario, they are much more willing to gamble on keeping the full $2,000.

As you can see, both options in both scenarios yield an expected utility of $1,500. However, they are framed very differently and feel very different psychologically. In the first scenario, the focus is on the possibility of gaining money from a reference point of $1,000. That is, it is a gain framework. In the second scenario, the focus is on the possibility of losing money from a reference point of $2,000, which is a loss framework. A wide variety of studies show this same pattern of results: people tend to be risk-averse in gain frameworks and risk-seeking in loss frameworks.

Prospect Theory (Figure 6.1)[28] provides us with a means of understanding this pattern of results. The horizontal axis represents gains and losses in currency. The vertical axis represents psychological value. In the positive direction, this means joy or happiness. In the negative direction, it means

Figure 6.1 Prospect Theory

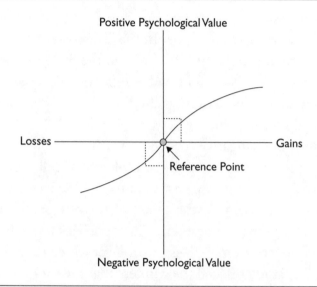

pain or sadness. As you can see in the figure, losses and gains are not experienced in the same way. Most importantly, the joy experienced from a gain is smaller in magnitude than the pain experienced from an equivalent loss. Stated another way, losses hurt us more than gains bring us joy.

There are other important things to note in the figure. As we pointed out, the psychological effects of gains and losses are not symmetrical, and prospect theory suggests that losses are weighted roughly twice as heavily as gains from an emotional standpoint. However, there is diminishing sensitivity as the numbers get bigger. Thus, the difference between $0 and $500 is much bigger psychologically than the difference between $10,000 and $10,500.

The most important thing to note is that gains and losses are valued relative to a reference point. In the first scenario described, the reference point is $1,000 and the $500 in question resides on the gain side of the figure. People tend to be more conservative here, opting to lock in gains and experience the associated joy. In the second scenario, however, the reference point is $2,000 and the $500 in question resides on the loss side. The fact that people feel losses more intensely makes them more willing to take a risk in order to avoid feeling the pain.

A study following investors over a five-year period revealed that people were significantly more likely to sell their winning stocks, locking in gains, than to sell their losers.[29] By holding onto losers, investors are effectively gambling on the possibility that these stocks will come back to some arbitrary reference point, such as the price at which they bought them. The study tracked the winners that investors sold and compared their returns to those of the losers that were held onto. At three months, one year, and two years out, the winners that were sold significantly outperformed the losers that investors hung on to. In this analysis, the bias toward locking in gains actually cost investors significant potential returns.

Does this suggest that you should advise your clients to sell all their losers and keep all their winners? Of course not. It does suggest that, all things being equal, clients enjoy locking in gains while keeping bad stocks too long in the hope of a recovery. This pattern also lends insight into the panic-selling phenomenon. When the market takes a sharp downward turn, many investors rush to sell their stock in order to lock in gains before prices sink further. Thus, mass selling fueled by individual loss aversion can spark wider declines that ultimately cost everybody in the market.

Clearly, the reference point that clients use is critical to their interpretation of performance and their resulting behavior. Left to their own devices, who knows what reference point clients will use? It could be peaks, valleys, where they bought the stock, where they expected it to be, the lofty returns advertised by the best-performing funds, or whatever. If a client's portfolio returns −10 percent this year, many will interpret that as a loss. If the broader markets return −20 percent and these indexes are the reference point, perhaps a 10 percent loss could be interpreted as a gain. The point is that you have influence on how clients set these reference points. It is critical that you help set proper and realistic reference points for your clients.

THE POWER OF FRAMING AND EMOTIONS

The previous section demonstrates that the way information is framed can have a dramatic impact on its interpretation and on the resulting behavior. The lesson is that the way information is presented can have a powerful effect. Furthermore, the way information is framed relative to time can also have a strong impact. For example, *myopic loss aversion* is the phenomenon that people become more loss-averse, risk-averse, and conservative in the near term, but less conservative when time horizons are longer. The results of one study showed that when investors viewed past returns in long-term increments, they chose much riskier allocations than they did if they viewed returns in short-term increments.[30] Results showed that when investors viewed monthly returns, they allocated just over 40 percent of their portfolio to stocks. When they viewed annual returns, they allocated nearly 70 percent to stocks. The returns represented the exact same information, but it was framed differently.

A naturally occurring frame that has tremendous impact on how clients make decisions stems from how people view time. There are fundamental differences in how clients construe the distant future versus the present.[31] Individuals tend to think of the distant future as being more abstract than the present. When they consider actions in the distant future, they tend to look at the bigger picture and consider *why* or why not they might undertake an action. A decision in the distant future is likely to be based on actual preferences, and there is a tendency to take a risk and give something a try. In contrast, when people consider actions in the present, they tend to be more concrete and focused on the details associated with the action and *how* they might actually undertake it. The decision is likely to be based on how feasible the action is and whether it is worth the effort. As a result, less risky courses of action tend to be preferred in the present.

As an example, imagine that you are considering attending an executive education event at Wharton a year from now. As you consider it, you might focus on why attending such an event might be a good or bad idea, what you might learn by attending the class sessions, and how interesting the topic seems to you. Now, imagine that you committed to the event a year ago and tomorrow is the day you have to leave. Suddenly, issues of what to pack, when you need to leave for the airport, and how you are going to be sure that your clients are attended to while you are away become preeminent.

These differences in how we view present versus distant events have many implications for financial decisions. We find it hard to invest today because we are not sure how to begin. But in the future, it will be a great idea to start saving. We don't bother to refinance a loan to realize better terms because in the short run it requires a big investment of time and potentially a lot of hassles. In the abstract, it is great to do, but we just don't have the time or the energy today. The *Save More Tomorrow* plan described earlier helps individuals to overcome these effects associated with how time is construed. In general, precommitments to engage in actions help people to cope with these framing effects.

Temporal framing also has a strong effect on the payoffs that people seek. In general, people prefer smaller immediate payoffs over larger payoffs for which they have to wait. However, when the choice is in the distant future, they clearly prefer larger payoffs. This is called *hyperbolic discounting* because the immediate reward often comes at a huge discount compared to waiting. For example, would you rather have $10 today or $11 tomorrow? Logic dictates that $11 tomorrow is much better (a 10 percent one-day return!), but people consistently choose $10 today. In contrast, would you rather have $10 in one year or $11 in one year plus one day? Here people consistently choose to wait the extra day and take the $11.

Over the years, this problem has sparked dozens of studies and multiple explanations. Recently, a team of researchers observed individuals who were presented with this type of problem while they were in a functional MRI machine.[32] This enabled the researchers to monitor the brain activity of the subjects while they considered the options. When people were presented with the near-term choice in which they hyperbolically discounted and chose the immediate smaller payoff, there was substantial activity in the emotional centers of their brains. However, when they were presented with the choice between payoffs in the distant future, they chose the larger payoff and had very little emotional activity. This is strong evidence that emotions are fueling these irrational near-term trade-offs.

Of course, emotions affect many consumer decisions and notably many financial decisions. We often hear from the advisors we work with that they are in the business of helping their clients to manage their emotions better so that they can make better financial decisions. When the advisors refer to specific emotions, they tend to focus on fear, regret, and anxiety, and they tend to lump all of these emotions together. This suggests that these negative emotions all have the same undesirable effects on client decision making. In reality, these emotions are quite distinct from one another and can have very different implications.

Anxiety, for example, biases consumers toward low-risk/low-reward options.[33] Anxiety occurs when people are uncertain about a personally relevant outcome and feel that they have low control over a situation, especially one that has potentially harmful implications. This heightens their preoccupation with avoiding losses and encourages them to adopt a more prevention-oriented mindset. One way to combat the effect of anxiety is to help increase the client's sense of control over the situation. In contrast, imagine a client who has recently inherited money as a result of the death of a family member and is coping with a deep sense of sadness. In general, *sadness* occurs when people feel the loss of a cherished object or person. It makes individuals want to replace what is missing with another type of reward. Feelings of sadness can heighten a preoccupation with reward and actually prompt a client to be less prudent with his inheritance than he should be. He might decide to take the money and splurge on something rewarding that might reduce his sadness.

Anger and *fear* are associated with other behaviors. To better understand this, consider the classic gain/loss scenario called the "Asian disease problem."[34] Imagine that the United States is preparing for the outbreak of an unusual Asian disease that is expected to kill 600 people. Two alternative programs to combat the disease are proposed. Under the gain frame, study participants are asked to consider Program A, in which 200 people will be saved, or Program B, in which there is a 1/3 probability that 600 people will be saved and a 2/3 probability that no one will be saved. Note that the expected values for Program A and Program B are equivalent at 200 people saved. Most participants prefer Program A, which ensures saving 200 lives. In the loss frame, study participants are asked to consider Program C, in which 400 people will die, or Program D, in which there is a 1/3 probability that nobody will die and a 2/3 probability that 600 people will die. Note that again the expected values for Program C and Program D are equivalent at 400 dead people. Given this choice, most participants prefer Program D, the risky choice. Note also that in all the scenarios, 200 people will be saved and 400 people will die. Also, these are the results we would expect based on prospect theory.

Now add anger and fear to this problem.[35] If we prompt people to feel angry, we find that they are risk-seeking across all frames, preferring the probabilistic option in both the gain and the loss framing. Anger encourages people to reach out and take a chance. In contrast, if we prompt people to feel fearful, they are risk-averse across all frames, preferring the sure options in both the gain and the loss framing. Most theoretical models of risk taking assume that risky decision making is a mostly cognitive process. However, we know from recent research that emotions often play a central role in decision making under uncertainty. Some emotions make individuals more likely to make risky decisions, while other emotions make them less likely to do so. In particular, this research suggests that not all negative emotions lead to the same behaviors on the part of investors.

We do know, however, that when clients perceive that time is short, they become particularly focused on avoiding situations that might lead to negative emotions and hence prefer to avoid losses.[36] They are also more receptive to advertising messages that position products or services as helping to avoid negative emotional outcomes. In contrast, when clients perceive that they have a long time horizon, they become more focused on achieving positive emotional outcomes and prefer to seek gains. They are also responsive to advertising messages that position products or services as helping to achieve positive emotional outcomes.

MENTAL ACCOUNTING

Mental accounting is a process by which consumers categorize their money and spending, allocating the debits and credits to different psychological accounts.[37] Importantly, research in this domain has found that these categories are notional and nonfungible. That is, money that has been allocated to one mental account is not a perfect substitute for money in another such account. As a result, money is coded as belonging in a specific category, and changes in the amount of money in that category are coded as gains or losses specifically within that category rather than as part of one's overall financial standing. People commonly refer to this as "coffee can accounting," referring to the old practice of placing cash for different purposes, like bill paying, savings, and fun, into different containers.

This process of mental accounting has important implications for client behavior. For example, it can explain why a client might maintain a balance in her savings account and at the same time pay 15 percent interest on balances maintained on a credit card. You will often hear these clients say something like, "But my savings is different. It's for a rainy day. I can't use that money to pay off my credit card balances."

A large body of research in psychology and marketing has identified different mindsets or strategies by which individuals pursue their goals.[38] These mindsets also have implications for the accounts to which clients might allocate their finances. To understand these different mindsets, consider two students who want to achieve an A grade in a course.[39] One student might pursue this goal by being approach-oriented. This student might take on a so-called promotion or eager strategy in pursuit of the A. The student might read beyond the required assignments or do other additional work in a quest to learn as much as possible. This promotion strategy is more likely to be used in the pursuit of goals related to advancement and accomplishment. Individuals who adopt such a strategy are focused on realizing gains and opportunities. In contrast, the other student might pursue an A grade by a more avoidance-oriented strategy. This student might be more prevention-focused and vigilant, making sure not to miss any deadlines or assignments. A prevention strategy is more likely to be used in the pursuit of goals related to security and protection. Individuals who adopt such a strategy are focused on avoiding losses and minimizing mistakes. The goal is the same, but the path to achieving the goal and the specific actions undertaken might be quite different.

Are there parallel behaviors among investors and students? Do you find that some of your clients are eager and gain-focused, while others are vigilant and loss-focused? They probably differ in the strategies by which they pursue their goals. This can be a stable personality difference. However, the same investor can pursue different goals across different types of investment options.

While the potential risks and returns from a specific financial option should ideally be evaluated simultaneously when deciding whether or not to choose that option, clients in fact often separate the risks and the returns into separate mental accounts: *promotion* and *prevention* accounts. In fact, some research has found that financial products themselves can trigger these different goals.[40] Thus, common stocks and trading accounts trigger promotion mindsets and make consumers more eager and more gain seeking. These types of investments are associated with pursuing goals that the consumer wants to achieve. In contrast, CDs and IRAs trigger more prevention mindsets and make consumers more vigilant and loss-focused. These types of products are associated with protection and safety. Consumers become more concerned with risk seeking in their trading accounts and more conservative with their IRAs. Thus, framing an investment as "retirement" can activate the concept of prevention, making investors too conservative when dealing with money invested over a long time horizon. The authors of this research also suggest that this perspective helps explain the opposition to the privatization of social security. If social security is associated with prevention mindsets such as vigilance, safety, and avoiding mistakes, any gains that might be realized through private investments in the stock market seem less important than preventing any risky losses.

WHAT CAN AN ADVISOR DO?

While having a clear understanding of investor psychology can help you educate your clients, it is unlikely that you can completely eliminate their systematic biases. Unfortunately, these biases are rooted deep in our cognitive systems, and although awareness can help us to avoid them, it does not cure us of them. So what is an advisor to do? With the knowledge of how investor psychology can bias decisions, you must create situations that diminish the impact of these biases or harness their effects. Here are some suggestions:

- *Combat complexity.* Simplification can be powerful and can help streamline decisions. Limiting choice sets and offering preset, age-based allocations can reduce complexity for your clients and make their decisions easier. However, be aware that clients are naturally drawn to large choice sets.

- *Harness inertia.* Don't fight inertia. Get it to work for you and your clients. Obtaining long-term commitments to future meetings, savings, and reallocations can change the psychological defaults and short-circuit procrastination.

- *Provide optimal framing.* Inventory your written and verbal communication. How are you presenting information to your clients? With compliance in mind,

you need to take a careful look at how your clients
are evaluating your performance and in what context.
Create reports that make the proper reference points
and comparisons explicit.

- *Understand temporal dynamics.* Again, your
  communication can focus clients on the present or the
  long term. Don't let myopia cloud your or your clients'
  judgments. Something as simple as presenting charts
  with yearly returns as opposed to monthly returns can
  completely change a client's perspective.

- *Manage emotions.* Investing is an emotional business.
  You can't expect your clients to be rational all the time,
  but you can help them set their emotions aside and
  make better decisions.

- *Manage across compartments.* Know that your clients
  use coffee can accounting. Help them see the big
  picture by creating reports and portfolios that span
  these mental compartments. Help them realize when
  they need to rethink their promotion- or prevention-
  oriented strategy.

A clearer understanding of investor psychology allows
you to better serve your clients. When you can frame information more appropriately and help clients make more
rational and maximizing decisions, you can help them create a better long-term strategy and hopefully achieve higher
returns. This understanding will help you create a clearer
path to success and will ultimately increase your value to
your clients.

NOTES

1. Dan Ariely, *Predictably Irrational* (New York: HarperCollins, 2008).

2. Jeremy J. Siegel, "The Resilience of American Finance," *Wall Street Journal*, September 16, 2008, p. A25.

3. Barry Schwartz, *The Paradox of Choice: Why More Is Less* (New York: HarperCollins, 2005).

4. Sheena S. Iyengar and Mark R. Lepper, "When Choice Is Demotivating: Can One Desire Too Much of a Good Thing?" *Journal of Personality and Social Psychology* 79, no. 6 (December 2000), 995–1006.

5. Gur Huberman, Sheena Iyengar, and Wei Jiang, "Defined Contribution Pension Plans: Determinants of Participation and Contributions Rates," *Journal of Financial Services Research* 31, no. 1 (February 2007), 1–32.

6. Schwartz, *The Paradox of Choice*.

7. Securities Investor Protection Corporation and Investor Protection Trust. *Investor Survival Skills Survey: An Examination of Investor Knowledge and Behavior*, prepared by Opinion Research Corporation, 2005.

8. John Hancock Financial Services, *Eighth Defined Contribution Plan Survey: Insights into Participant Investment Knowledge and Behavior*, 2002.

9. Barclay's Global Investors, *Measuring Affluent and HNW Investor Expectations of the Investment and Financial Community*, report prepared by Cogent Research for iShares, March 2008.

10. Brad Barber and Terrance Odean, "Boys Will Be Boys: Gender, Overconfidence, and Common Stock Investment," *Quarterly Journal of Economics* 116, no. 1 (February 2001), 261–292.

11. Brad Barber and Terrance Odean, "Trading Is Hazardous to Your Wealth: The Common Stock Investment Performance of Individual Investors," *Journal of Finance* 55, no. 2 (April 2000), 773–806.

12. D. Kahneman, P. Slovic, and A. Tversky, *Judgment under Uncertainty: Heuristics and Biases* (New York: Cambridge University Press, 1982).

13. Olivia S. Mitchell and Stephen P. Utkus, *Pension Design and Structure: New Lessons from Behavioral Finance* (Oxford and New York: Oxford University Press, 2004).

14. Brad Barber and Terrance Odean, "All That Glitters: The Effect of Attention and News on the Buying Behavior of Individual and Institutional Investors," *Review of Financial Studies* 21, no. 2 (March 2008), 785–818.

15. Kahneman, Slovic, and Tversky, *Judgment under Uncertainty*.

16. Richard Deaves, "Data-Conditioning Biases, Performance, Persistence and Flows: The Case of Canadian Equity Funds," *Journal of Banking & Finance* 28, no. 3 (March 2004), 673–695.

17. Daniel Read and George Loewenstein, "Diversification Bias: Explaining the Discrepancy in Variety Seeking between Combined and Separated Choices," *Journal of Experimental Psychology* 1, no. 4 (1995), 34–49.

18. Shlomo Benartzi and Richard H. Thaler, "Naïve Diversification Strategies in Defined Contribution Saving Plans," *American Economic Review* 91, no. 1 (March 2001), 79–98.

19. William Samuelson and Richard J. Zeckhauser, "Status Quo Bias in Decision Making," *Journal of Risk and Uncertainty* 1 (1988), 7–59.

20. Barry Staw, "Knee Deep in the Big Muddy," *Organizational Behavior and Human Performance* 16, no. 4 (1976), 27–44.

21. See Kahneman, Slovic, and Tversky, *Judgment under Uncertainty*.

22. E. J. Johnson, J. Hershey, J. Meszaros, and H. Kunreuther, "Framing, Probability Distortions, and Insurance Decisions," *Journal of Risk and Uncertainty* 7 (1993), 35–51.

23. James J. Choi, David Laibson, Brigitte C. Madrian, and Andrew Metrick. *For Better or for Worse: Default Effects and 401(k) Savings Behavior*, National Bureau of Economic Research Working Paper no. 8651, December 2001.

24. Brigitte Madrian and Dennis Shea, "The Power of Suggestion: Inertia in 401(k) Participation and Savings Behavior," *Quarterly Journal of Economics* 116, no. 4 (November 2001), 1149–1187.

25. Richard H. Thaler and Shlomo Benartzi, "Save More Tomorrow: Using Behavioral Economics to Increase Employee Saving," *Journal of Political Economy* 112, no. 1 (February 2004), 164–187.

26. Dilip Soman, George Ainslie, Shane Frederick, et al., "The Psychology of Intertemporal Discounting: Why Are Distant Events Valued Differently from Proximal Ones?" *Marketing Letters* 16, no. 3 (December 2005), 347–360.

27. Daniel Kahneman and Amos Tversky, "Prospect Theory: An Analysis of Decisions under Risk, *Econometrica* 46 (1979), 171–185.

28. Ibid.

29. Terrance Odean, "Are Investors Reluctant to Realize Their Losses?" *Journal of Finance* 53, no. 5 (October 1998), 1775–1798.

30. Richard Thaler, Amos Tversky, and Daniel Kahneman, "The Effect of Myopia and Loss Aversion on Risk Taking: An Experimental Test," *Quarterly Journal of Economics* 112, no. 2 (May 1997), 647–661.

31. Tal Eyal, Nira Liberman, Yaacov Trope, and Eva Walther, "The Pros and Cons of Temporally Near and Distant Action," *Journal of Personality and Social Psychology* 86, no. 6 (June 2004), 781–795.

32. Samuel M. McClure, David I. Laibson, George Loewenstein, and Jonathan D. Cohen, "Separate Neural Systems Value Immediate and Delayed Monetary Rewards," *Science* 306 (October 2004), 503–507.

33. Rajagopal Raghunathan and Michel Tuan Pham, "All Negative Moods Are Not Equal: Motivational Influences of Anxiety and Sadness on Decision Making," *Organizational Behavior and Human Decision Processes* 79, no. 1 (July 1999), 56–77.

34. A. Tversky and D. Kahneman, "The Framing of Decisions and the Psychology of Choice," *Science* 211 (1981), 453–458.

35. J. S. Lerner and D. Keltner, "Fear, Anger, and Risk," *Journal of Personality and Social Psychology* 81, no. 1 (2001), 146–159.

36. Patti Williams and A. Drolet, "Age-Related Differences in Responses to Emotional Advertisements," *Journal of Consumer Research* 32 (December 2005), 343–354.

37. Richard H. Thaler, "Mental Accounting Matters," *Journal of Behavioral Decision Making* 12, no. 3 (1999), 183–206.

38. E. T. Higgins, "Beyond Pleasure and Pain," *American Psychologist* 52, no. 12 (1997), 1280–1300.

39. Michel Tuan Pham and E. Tory Higgins, "Promotion and Prevention in Consumer Decision Making: State of the Art and Theoretical Propositions," in S. Ratneshwar and David Glen Mick (eds.), *Inside Consumption: Frontiers of Research on Consumer Motives, Goals, and Desires* (London: Routledge, 2004).

40. Rongrong Zhou and Michel Tuan Pham, "Promotion and Prevention across Mental Accounts: When Financial Products Dictate Consumers' Investment Goals," *Journal of Consumer Research* 31, no. 1 (June 2004), 125–135.

CHAPTER 7

QUANTITATIVE CLIENT RELATIONSHIP MANAGEMENT

Clients are different and require different actions. A discipline called client relationship management (CRM[1]) is based on this simple fact. CRM refers to the practices of firms and the set of tools they use to recognize that clients are different and require different actions, both overall and at different times during their relationship with you. The success that you have as a financial advisor rests solely on your ability to manage your relationships with your clients. For some advisors, the first step is the mere recognition that what you have with your clients is, in fact, a *relationship*. Your relationship with your clients is where your practice begins, continues, and ends.

It would be trite to say, "Pay attention to your clients!" and that is not what CRM is about. Rather, how many financial advisors have taken a systematic and *quantitative* look at their clients? Do you have the correct mix of clients? Do you have too many clients? Believe it or not, that is possible. In fact, our survey data suggest that the average financial advisor should have no more than 75 to 100 *major* clients at any one time. We will expand on this later when we talk about the details of CRM. Does each of your clients provide a positive net present value (NPV), that is, a financial return to your practice, and how do you know this? Which of your clients have strategic value and may be able to act as word-of-mouth ambassadors (see Chapter 1)? We describe CRM techniques and concepts using a stylized (yet realistic) example. Note that we call this chapter quantitative CRM because our focus here is on the quantitative ways in which client management can be improved with data. There is an entire other set of CRM "skills" that are more behavioral in nature, and those are covered in other parts of this book.

COMPUTING CUSTOMER LIFETIME VALUE AND ITS ASSOCIATED METRICS

Imagine a financial services advisor with five types of clients/prospects: ultra-high-net-worth, large, medium, small, and prospects, as summarized in Figures 7.1 and 7.2, which give data for a "healthy" and a "struggling" practice, respectively. We call these Firm A and Firm B for convenience. Let us analyze the two firms closely and see what is similar and what separates them. This is the kind of client assessment that should be part of CRM and part of your five Cs (customer, client, competitor, collaborator, and context) analysis described in Chapter 1. The six column variables selected represent those decision variables that are commonly used both in the financial services industry to evaluate clients and also in the customer lifetime value (CLV) literature[2] that is pervasive in marketing.[3]

Figure 7.1 Firm A: Profile of a Healthy Financial Services Practice

	Average Asset Value under Management per Client	Number of Clients	Yearly Revenue Generation per Client	Acquisition Costs per Client	Annual Retention Cost per Client	Strategic Importance of Each Client
Ultra-high	$11 million	8	$220,000	$400,000	$12,000	High
Large	$2 million	17	$32,000	$60,000	$5,000	High
Medium	$1 million	34	$15,000	$25,000	$3,000	Medium
Small	$250,000	21	$4,000	$3,000	$500	Low
Prospects	$0	100	$0	$40,000	$4,000	Medium

Figure 7.2 Firm B: Profile of a Struggling Financial Services Practice

	Average Asset Value under Management per Client	Number of Clients	Yearly Revenue Generation per Client	Acquisition Costs per Client	Annual Retention Cost per Client	Strategic Importance of Each Client
Ultra-high	$11 million	4	$170,000	$400,000	$40,000	High
Large	$2 million	25	$25,000	$75,000	$10,000	High
Medium	$1 million	60	$15,000	$40,000	$7,000	Medium
Small	$250,000	55	$3,000	$4,000	$1,000	Low
Prospects	$0	200	$0	$50,000	$8,000	Medium

While these two tables seem innocuous, let us stress that we could write an entire book just about them. Thus, let us go over the salient comparative statistics of each, which tell a very interesting story about how one should evaluate one's client base.

Number of Clients

Most people want to start by looking at the number of active clients. If we add up just the number of active clients, we see that Firm A has 80 active clients, whereas Firm B has 144.

Which would you rather be? Many people might quickly say, Firm B. However, number of clients is a poor measure of success and can lead to suboptimal acquisition strategies. The change in the number of clients is more relevant. Furthermore, having a true customer relationship with 144 unique clients is extremely difficult. Thus, having a lot of clients who share common characteristics that match your strengths is good, as we discussed in Chapters 2 and 3, but client acquisition for numbers' sake is likely to lead to poor service for all of them.

Assets under Management

Assets under management is also a common metric of success. If we compute this for Firm A, we see that it has $161.25 million, whereas Firm B has $167.75 million, a slight advantage. While this is not a bad thing for Firm B, what is more relevant is how much revenue is being generated from the assets under management, and at what cost. Furthermore, when we compute assets under management on a per client basis, we see that Firm A has $2.01 million under management per client as compared to $1.165 million for Firm B (a nearly 80 percent increase). As we discuss later, this may very well have both short- and long-term benefits for Firm A. However, before you get the wrong impression, we are not saying that Firm B is necessarily wrong to have higher assets under management. We are saying that it is crucial that you grow your assets under management in a smart way. Furthermore, no one is suggesting that you must bankrupt the firm and start from scratch to implement this approach. Rather, it is about the proper allocation of effort going forward.

Revenue Generation

When we compute the amount of revenue generated by Firm A and by Firm B, we see an entirely different story. Firm A is generating $2.898 million in revenue, whereas Firm B is generating $2.37 million. This is a good sign for Firm A for a multitude of reasons.

First, Firm A is generating almost 30 percent more revenue from almost 40 percent fewer clients. This indicates that Firm A probably has a larger dollar wallet share[4] of its clients' assets than Firm B does, suggesting a better relationship between Firm A's financial advisors and its clients. In fact, one of the tactics that we will discuss in detail is that gaining additional dollars from existing clients is much easier and has lower acquisition costs than acquiring new clients. Thus, as our survey data show, the most successful financial advisors spend more time on client retention than on acquisition—except, of course, when trying to penetrate a new segment or to obtain a few select strategically and financially valuable clients.

Second, and equally important, a larger fraction of dollar wallet share leads to greater loyalty. The likelihood of client churn (moving to a different financial advisor or firm) is inversely related to the dollar wallet share that you have under management; this could be the result of an improved relationship with the client or simply higher switching costs to move a larger amount of assets. Either way, dollar wallet share is a metric that should be in every financial advisor's tool kit and is a much better metric of success than purely the amount of assets under management. In other words, $1 million out of $10 million is not the same as $1 million out of $100 million. So, starting a dialogue with your clients to understand how you can serve them better is one of the tactics that we discuss in Chapter 9.

Cost of Acquisition

Acquisition costs are those expenses that are accrued before the first dollar under asset management appears. These costs of doing business need to be thought of more broadly than just actual dollars spent (e.g., dinners, social outings with clients, and so on); they must include human labor costs (your and your staff's time) that are attributable to acquiring a client. This, of course, requires you to understand the value of time for each individual associated with an organization, including support staff, and a method for collecting such data. In particular, do you record how much time you spend with a client? Do the members of your staff? Each of these cost items is crucial for enabling you to understand which clients are most valuable. This is discussed further later in this chapter. As an example of such cost accounting practices, we all have potentially a lot to learn on this dimension from legal practices. This is not to say that a legal firm pricing model is appropriate for your practice, but rather that the equating of time and "value/fees" is a useful mindset to have.

Returning to Firms A and B, Firm A has total acquisition costs of $5.133 million compared to $6.095 million for Firm B. So, not only does Firm A have lower total costs of acquisition than Firm B, but it is also generating more revenue as a result. Furthermore, and this is also diagnostic, Firm A has lower acquisition costs for all client types except ultra-high-net-worth clients. Lower acquisition costs are a strong signal that Firm A might be better at converting prospects to actual clients, which is one evaluative diagnostic that every firm should understand. To expand on this, do you keep records of every initial client meeting that you have? Do you keep records of how many of them convert to second meetings and to eventual clients? This process is related to the famous statement, "You are only as strong as your weakest link." That is, it is very insightful to understand which aspect of your practice needs the most improvement. Do you have lots of initial meetings, but very few follow-ups? Do you have many follow-ups, but few conversions? Are you able to convert prospects to clients well, but not retain them well? These are the types of statistics that you should track.

Annual Retention Costs and Yearly Profitability

Let us not forget that most firms are in the business of profit optimization, not revenue optimization or cost minimization. It is the combination of robust revenue and a clear understanding of cost drivers that allows firms to be profitable. Not surprisingly, given that Firm A has higher total annual revenue and lower annual retention costs ($293,500 versus $885,000), it will have greater annual profits. Furthermore, when we look at the retention costs per client for Firms A and B, we notice again that Firm A's retention costs are much lower for each client type. Thus, while Firm B appears to be able to acquire clients, it is unable to hold them as well as Firm A does, or at least it has to pay more to try to do so. When we discuss CLV, we will see the critical role that customer retention plays in the value of clients over a long-term time horizon.

Payback Period

While this example is hypothetical, it is indeed realistic in most respects. One particular aspect that was intentionally chosen this way, and is consistent with many extant industry reports, is the amount of time it takes to recoup the acquisition costs. Notice that for both Firms A and B (except for the small customers for Firm A), the acquisition costs for each client type are greater than the annualized average revenue. This suggests a payback period of more than a year to hit breakeven revenue.[5] Thus, if a firm acquires clients who do not stay for very long, then, in fact, those customers will have negative profit implications for the firm. While this should be obvious, the relevance of the payback period is often forgotten. When you are just starting out and you need to acquire a certain amount of revenue, profitability, and clients within a certain time period, then the payback period may be the most important thing to you. It may be even more important than the lifetime value described next, which you may never see because you could be out of business by then. Furthermore, you certainly might behave very differently if you know that it will take three or four years of assets under management just to break even on the cost of acquiring a client.

Customer Lifetime Value and Firing Clients

To motivate this section, let us ask an apparently innocuous question followed by a quiz:

If you wanted to rank-order your clients from most to least important, what would you rank them on?

Would your answer be assets under management? Would it be yearly profitability? Would it be strategic importance?

While each of these answers is a *component* and plays an important role, when viewed individually, they fail to take a holistic view of clients. Hence, each of these answers individually is wrong.

Instead, consider the following general framework. Acquiring a client costs money. That client generates a yearly revenue stream that is likely to vary over time, has a probability of churn in each and every year, has associated yearly retention costs, and has a strategic value that can help bring in other clients. It is the combination of all of these factors that determines the value of a client. In marketing lingo, we call this value the *client lifetime value*, which is the discounted net present value that a client will bring in over her lifetime with you as a client. Simply put, you should compute this for each and every client. Furthermore, trying to compute the component pieces will force you to think systematically and quantitatively about your clients. Even if some of these numbers are approximate (e.g., cost information on a per client basis), just thinking about generating them will help you to better understand and prioritize your customers.

Putting all of the aforementioned words together, formulaically, leads to the expression for the CLV of a customer given in Figure 7.3.

As mentioned earlier, C_0, the acquisition cost of a customer, drives down the CLV, as these are initial start-up expenses that need to be recaptured. A natural assumption, therefore, is that it is best for your firm if acquisition costs are as low as possible, right? Not necessarily. Acquisition

Figure 7.3 Computation of Customer Lifetime Value: How Much Is That Customer Worth?

$$CLV = -C_0 + \Sigma_{t=1}^{T} \frac{(R_t - C_t + S_t) \times P_t}{(1+r)^t}$$

where C_0 = customer acquisition cost

C_t = retention cost at time t

P_t = probability that the given client is still your client at time t

R_t = revenue generated by the client in time period t

S_t = strategic value of the client

r = time value of money

T = time horizon

costs are a "strange animal." Generally, you want your acquisition costs to be low when you are trying to acquire customers, but you want those of other firms to be high (i.e., you want to have low acquisition costs but high switching costs). Of course, one major purpose and thrust of this book is that through better branding and client relationship management, you can drive up switching costs.

Next, C_t is the yearly costs at time t that must be spent to retain a given customer. These typically would include face-to-face meeting time, thank-you events, dinners, costs of promotional materials, and other expenses that must be covered on a yearly basis. The common name for these, and it is apropos, is retention costs. Driving down retention costs should be one major goal of any financial advisor, and this is where segmentation (as described in Chapters 2 and 3) plays a significant role. A better STP strategy will enable you to be efficient and maintain higher retention at lower cost.

The next element, P_t, is one that is commonly ignored, but that is the perhaps the *most* important driver of CLV:

likelihood of client retention. In particular, P_1 is the probability that a given client will still be a client in a year, P_2 is the probability that he will still be a client two years hence, and so on. This appropriately reflects the fact that clients churn, you should expect that they will churn and, most importantly, clients do not all have an equal probability of churning. The question is, how do you estimate P_t? There are two basic ways that are used in practice—one that is straight empirical, and one that requires more sophisticated statistical modeling (which we discuss only briefly).

The empirical way to estimate churn rates is what you would naturally expect. Of the clients you acquire, what fraction are still your clients one year from the date of acquisition? That gives you an estimate of P_1. What fraction are still your clients at the end of year 2? That gives you an estimate of P_2, and so on. A reasonable question to ask is, why do you ever need more than this empirical approach? Shouldn't these historical data be the best predictor of client churn rates going forward? There are at least two reasons why you might want something more. First, imagine that you have acquired 100 clients over the last five years (the data you will use to compute P_t). How can you estimate P_6? You have no data on clients for six years. Or, imagine that you have only five clients who stayed until their fifth year. How confident would you feel about your estimates of P_5 and later values? Not very, because you just do not have enough data. Second, suppose you wanted to estimate client churn as a function of the age of your clients, their assets under management, or other factors. A straight empirical approach does not provide that level of detail.

An alternative approach to estimating churn rates is called *hazard modeling*.[6] Hazard modeling is a series of techniques that have been developed primarily in biostatistics (where the hazard is literally death) and engineering (where the hazard might be the failure of a joint or safety system). The analogy to financial services is direct. Here, the hazard is churning or clients leaving your practice. The way hazard modeling works is that you model the probability that, given that someone has not churned by year t, she will churn in year $t + 1$. For example, imagine that 100 clients are acquired in year 1, 80 of them remain in year 2, 55 of them in year 3, 20 of them in year 4, and none of them in year 5. Then the corresponding empirical hazard rates would be 20 percent for year 1 (of the 100 you started with, 20 percent churned), 31.3 percent for year 2 (of the 80 you started with, 55 or 68.7 percent remain), 63.7 percent for year 3, and 100 percent for year 4, respectively. Thus, as we can see, the hazard rate provides detailed information about the derivative or steepness of the drop-off in any given year.

When these data are collected on the individual client level, then one can relate the time of churn to specific characteristics of the client. This allows you to answer questions such as, "Do larger clients churn faster?" While it is beyond the direct scope of this book to provide details, hazard modeling of your customer churn rates is worth the analytic cost of learning and can be done with standard statistical software packages.

Similarly, R_t is the revenue that you can expect from a given client over time. R_t can be thought of and estimated in the same way as P_t. That is, you can compute empirical revenue curves for customers or model them (now not hazard curves, but revenue curves) in some way. Note the business value of understanding R_t. Do your clients provide more revenue for you over time? If not, this is one symptom of a firm that can use improvement. Measuring R_t over time is clearly related to dollar wallet share, which was discussed earlier.

S_t can be thought of as the "social network value" that will accrue from other clients because of the fact that this person is currently a client. This may not be easy to measure; however, keeping track of referrals is one way to approach estimating this. This is why in Figures 7.1 and 7.2, we simply categorize that value as high, medium, or low. Of course, this will have to be quantified eventually. Although this is somewhat speculative, we suggest that the best way to think about S_t is as a percentage of that client's value of R_t. So, for instance, if this is a highly strategically valued client, one could imagine that $S_t = 3$ to $5 \times R_t$. Then, modeling R_t gives one a way to determine the value of S_t. Of course, another approach is to compute CLV as given in Figure 7.3 ignoring S_t, but giving a bump at the end to a client with a high strategic value: $CLV_{new} = 3$ to $5 \times CLV$.

While it is difficult to quantify, strategic value is something that it is worth the time to assess. As we have discussed throughout the book, this is a referral-driven business. Thus, the importance of strategic value is high compared to other industries. The potential for a client to become a word-of-mouth ambassador must be considered. For instance, is the client a member of many affinity groups? Is she very active in her church? Is she highly socially networked? Word of mouth tends to flow through opinion leaders and people who are at the center of their social network. Additionally, word flows much more easily within groups than between groups. Hence, a client with low monetary value may have high strategic value. It is crucial to assess this value and weight CLV appropriately.

Finally, r is the time discount factor that recognizes that a dollar tomorrow is not worth the same amount as a dollar today. For instance, if you could put a dollar today into a risk-free asset and get a guaranteed 7 percent return, then a dollar tomorrow is not worth a dollar today, but rather $1/(1.07)$ today. A dollar two years from now is not worth $1 today; rather, it is worth $1/(1.07)^2$ today, and so on. This is why the CLV equation presented in Figure 7.3 discounts each year's expected profit stream by the time value of money. Additionally, T is the time horizon over which you would like to compute the CLV for your customers. This could be 5 years, 10 years, 20 years, or possibly an infinite number of years. While the values of r and T that are selected are often driven by internal corporate standards (or empirically by how long clients tend to stay), needless to say, a higher r will lower the CLV of a customer, as will a lower selected T, the time horizon over which we count the revenue stream.

We end this section on CLV with a brief discussion of "firing clients," as this is one of the key tools of client relationship management. Simply put, there are many clients for whom the value computed in Figure 7.3 is negative. That is, when their acquisition costs, yearly retention costs, and strategic value are taken into account, their expected revenue simply is not likely to outweigh their costs. Hence, even though the client is indeed generating positive revenue, his CLV is negative. The number of these clients needs to be reduced or eliminated. As unnatural as it may sound, every successful firm has to recognize that some clients are too costly to keep. For some clients, their CLV may be positive, but the investment they require prevents the firm from achieving a more positive return from others. The question, though, is how to reduce or eliminate these customers?

One option, which we recommend only in very severe situations, is to literally tell clients that you do not want their business anymore. This is severe not so much because of the loss of assets under management, but because of the potential damage to your brand as a result of negative word of mouth. Most clients who are literally fired may go out of their way to damage your reputation, and, as the old saying goes, it takes a lifetime to build a good reputation, but it can be gone in an instant. If you must take this action, you should make it clear that you do not feel that you are able to serve this client in the manner that she expects and that she will be better served by someone else. A very common alternative to this direct approach is to transfer the client to a more junior FA. Advisors in our survey most often use this tactic when trying to reduce the number of unprofitable clients.

A better option, which we suggest, is to let clients fire themselves by gradually reducing the level of service that you provide to them or by raising your fees. One of two things can result from this action. Perhaps the clients leave, and you are happy because they have chosen to leave themselves and hence have fired themselves. These customers will be much less likely to be negative toward you in the future, and if you have an exit interview and actually reach out to them for one last time, the likelihood of negative word of mouth will be even lower. Alternatively, if they choose to stay, you are also happy because you lowered your level of service to them or raised your revenue from them, resulting in a positive impact on CLV.

Client Mix

As stated earlier, while the number of clients is important to any practice, it is easy to argue that one's client mix (the distribution of clients over different size tiers) is more important. Looking at Firm A, we can see that approximately 80 percent of its revenue comes from its top 25 clients (31 percent of the client base), who are nested within the two largest asset tiers. In comparison, Firm B is generating only 55 percent of its revenue from the two largest asset tiers (29 clients, or 20 percent of its client base). Why is this advantageous for Firm A? First and foremost, clients in lower asset tiers are more likely to churn; hence, Firm A's assets under management and revenue stream are more protected. Second, Firm A has a more classic distribution of clients consistent with the famous "80–20" rule of marketing—that is, 80 percent of your revenues should (and typically do) come from 20 percent of your clients. In essence, loyalty and dollar wallet share are the key long-term success metrics. Firm A has a good balance; Firm B does not.

SUMMARY AND CONCLUSIONS

For some advisors, collecting and analyzing data and applying CLV techniques might seem to be a large stretch from where they are now. We suggest that you make that stretch. Brand and loyalty, and hence assets under management, revenues, and profits, are generated one client at a time. CLV methods can help you prioritize your clients, track them over time, determine the ROI of particular tactics that you are trying out, and, most importantly, provide a structured way of looking at your practice. Returning to the analogy mentioned earlier, the methods discussed in this chapter can help you determine your weakest link. Are you generating sufficient revenues (like Firm B), but your retention costs are so high that you are unable to generate sufficient profits? Are you able to retain customers well, but not to turn prospects into clients? In this case, improving your selling methods may be in order. Are you good at acquiring clients but poor at keeping them? What is the cause? Is it you? Is it your staff? Through CLV calculations, these questions can be answered rigorously, which is much more likely to lead to improved decisions that are not subject to the biases inherent in more subjective methods.

NOTES

1. CRM typically stands for customer relationship management, but in the sphere of financial advising, we refer to this as client relationship management.

2. Paul D. Berger and Nada I. Nasr, "Customer Lifetime Value: Marketing Models and Applications," *Journal of Interactive Marketing* 12, no. 1 (1998), 17–30.

3. The one key driver of CLV that is not given in these tables is churn rate. We discuss this in the section on the calculation of CLV.

4. Dollar wallet share refers to the fraction of a client's investable assets under management that a given firm has.

5. Breakeven revenue is the amount of client revenue needed to cover the initial acquisition costs. As in many industries, this can take more than a year.

6. Zainab Jamal and Randolph E. Bucklin, "Improving the Diagnosis and Prediction of Customer Churn: A Heterogeneous Hazard Modeling Approach," *Journal of Interactive Marketing* 20, no. 3/4 (Summer/Autumn 2006), 16–29.

CHAPTER 8

INTEGRATED MARKETING COMMUNICATIONS: MANAGING ADVERTISING, WEB SITE DESIGN, AND WORD OF MOUTH

A good marketing plan consists of the four Ps: product, price, place, and promotion. This chapter focuses specifically on the promotion P, or, more descriptively, on marketing communications.

When most people think of marketing, the first thing they think about is advertising. It is no surprise, then, that when most people think of marketing communications, they again first think of advertising. We hope to make it clear that marketing is a lot more than just advertising, especially in the financial services industry. Similarly, even marketing communications encompasses more than just advertising.

Marketing communication is "the voice of a brand and the means by which companies can establish a dialogue with consumers ... allow[ing] marketers to inform, persuade, incite and remind consumers."[1] The standard way of thinking about the promotion P today is to frame it within the context of *integrated marketing communications*, or IMC.

The IMC approach is much broader than a focus on just advertising (see Figure 8.1). It emphasizes that everything a brand does communicates something about itself to its market. Traditionally, advertising has dominated the communications function within most organizations. Other disciplines, such as public relations or direct marketing, were handled separately and were treated as second-class citizens in the overall brand-building arsenal. However, with media fragmentation and audience shrinkage in any given channel, there has been an increasing appreciation of the efficacy of nonadvertising tools. As a result, there has been an emphasis

Figure 8.1 The Integrated Marketing Communications Model

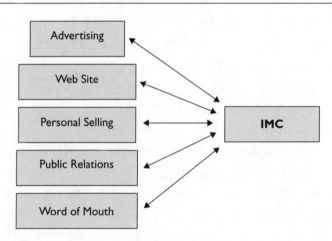

on developing a more strategic integration of all the communication alternatives that a brand might choose from.

The IMC approach argues that a firm should develop a communication strategy that uses all its marketing activities as opportunities to communicate the brand to its clients. As a result, each of these "touchpoints" should be carefully integrated to deliver a consistent, unified image. While a component of this is tactical, emphasizing a consistent look and voice across all communications channels, it is better conceived of as a strategic mission that identifies the most appropriate and effective channels, messages, and methods with which to communicate and build relationships with clients.[2] The idea is that while each communication opportunity has some impact on its own, together they have an interactive effect that is greater than the sum of the individual parts; hence the I in IMC. The effect of any communication option will depend, in part, on the communication effects created by all the other options. In addition, different communication options have different strengths and weaknesses.

IMC focuses on maximizing the joint benefits that accrue across the entire set of options, while minimizing their joint weaknesses. The benefits of one type of communication option can be put to use to make up for the weaknesses of another. As an example, traditional print and television advertising are relatively easy to buy and relatively intrusive, making it more likely that a marketer can use either of these options to get a potential client's attention. But they are one-way media that offer no opportunity for clients to ask questions and seek additional information (i.e., they are not interactive). A Web site, on the other hand, is much more interactive and can be designed to be responsive to a client's need for information, but it is not at all intrusive. Most clients get to an FA's Web site only by specifically navigating there. It's very useful once the client's attention has already been captured, but not at all useful beforehand. The IMC perspective makes it clear that marketers should realize these differences and use them to guide the nature of the messages sent out using these various options. An FA will want to use traditional advertising very differently from the way she will want to use her Web site. Each alternative should be put to its best use, and the entire bundle of alternatives should be considered together as a set of joint strategic decisions.

Each method of communication and each message that is sent must be integrated into the whole. It should be clear, for example, that your ads and your Web site are promoting the same brand. The visual design should be the same across communication vehicles. If your logo appears in the lower right-hand corner of your advertising, put it in the lower right-hand corner of your Web site, your business cards, your brochures, the notebooks you give your clients, and everywhere else it appears. Similarly, the way in which the brand is positioned should be integrated across all these communication options. The associations you are trying to build and the differentiating path you have chosen should be portrayed consistently in each message you deliver across every medium. You might emphasize different aspects in different channels, but ultimately your message in each medium should hang together in a structured fashion.

Like everything else we have discussed in this book, an integrated marketing communications plan begins with a comprehensive marketing strategy. Who is the target segment of clients that you wish to communicate with? What do you wish to tell them? How are you different from the competition? What promotion channels do the members of your target segment pay the most attention to? How are you uniquely relevant to their life goals? Once you know the answers to these questions, you can begin to develop a marketing communications strategy.

A good marketing communications plan focuses on providing answers to a handful of questions:

- *Whom* do you wish to communicate with?
- *What* do you wish to say to them?
- *What* do you want them to do?
- *How* can you best make these points?
- *Where* will you place these messages?

And of course, a budget for these objectives has to be specified. Underneath all of this should be a basic strategic framework, decided on in advance, specifying the objectives you have for your marketing communications efforts. What exactly do you want to accomplish through your marketing communications? Many marketers go wrong by not answering this question precisely enough.

Recently, an FA sent one of us an e-mail asking for advice about his marketing and communications goals. "My goal is to grow my business," he said. This is a reasonable goal, but one that is far too general. There are many ways in which he could grow his business.

- Did he want to grow his business by acquiring new clients?
- Did he want to acquire those new clients by encouraging word of mouth from existing clients?

- Or was he more focused on growth through expanded interactions (greater dollar wallet share) with existing clients?

- If the latter, did he want his current clients to buy a different or a broader assortment of products and services from him, to give him a greater percentage of their total assets to manage, or all of these?

- If he wished to get clients to try new products or services, which ones should he choose?

- What was his time horizon for this growth? Did he wish for it to happen over the next three months or over the next year?

- How much growth was he looking for?

- Did he want to acquire 10 new clients, 20 new clients, or more?

- Did he want to increase his assets under management by 5 percent, 10 percent, or 30 percent?

Good marketing objectives specify the target market and the time frame for accomplishing the goal. Good objectives are realistic and attainable, and they are quantifiable. It's important that the objectives lend themselves to realistic measures of success and that the marketer specify in advance how the impact of the marketing communications will be measured. That is, you as a small business are never absolved from thinking about or, even better, computing the return on investment (ROI) from your marketing expenditures.

The more precisely you specify your objectives for a particular marketing communications campaign, the more precisely you will be able to tailor your efforts to achieve those goals and the more precisely you will be able to measure the effectiveness of your efforts afterwards. After more careful consideration, this FA settled on a much more precise goal for himself: to grow his business by acquiring 10 high-net-worth clients in his target segment, which he had already identified, over the next 12 months. He defined high-net-worth clients as having liquid assets in excess of $10 million. He set a goal of acquiring five of those clients by encouraging word of mouth among his existing clients and five through his own sourcing. Because he had never set such specific goals before, he was reluctant to be any more focused than this. But a year from now, when he looks back at where and how he succeeded, he will have substantially more insight into what worked and what did not. He will be in a better position to specify objectives and allocate resources going forward.

The answer to the question about *who* starts with the choice of a target market. But, as suggested earlier, you might wish to narrow this even further. Are you speaking to potential clients within that target segment or to current clients? Are you speaking to current clients with the intention of educating them about new products and services, or perhaps with the intention of ultimately managing a larger share of their portfolio? Each of these groups will be receptive to different messages. Careful specification of your objectives, coupled with an understanding of the process by which these clients are likely to process your messages, is an important part of developing a marketing communications strategy.

Many marketers spend too little time here and, as a result, minimize the potential impact of their messages before they have even delivered those messages. You can't fully execute on *what* your message should say without a clear understanding of *whom* you are talking to and the kind of messages to which they will be most receptive. This means not only understanding their motivations for becoming your clients, but also understanding what they currently know and don't know about working with you. Their motivations and their current thoughts and feelings about you should be the starting point for the development of your messages.

When conceptualizing how receivers process and are persuaded by marketing communications, it is common to rely on models that depict a so-called "hierarchy of effects." In such a model, consumers are thought to pass through a series of phases in a sequential or hierarchical order. Though there are different versions of the hierarchy, essentially they all propose the continuum shown in Figure 8.2.

So, when learning about a new FA, a client must first become aware that the FA exists. As we stressed in Chapter 4, on branding, awareness is a necessary but not a sufficient condition for the establishment of a strong brand. Similarly, in the persuasion process, awareness is a necessary but not a sufficient condition for persuasion to occur. Once awareness has been achieved, consumers can start to develop knowledge about the FA. This knowledge might be the associations that the FA wishes to establish in the client's mind.

Awareness and knowledge are essentially cognitive stages, focused on educating the client about who the FA is and what she stands for. Those associations might in turn reflect how the FA is particularly relevant to the client's own needs

Figure 8.2 The Process of Persuasion for an IMC Program

| Unaware | Awareness | Knowledge | Liking | Conviction | Action |

and objectives, and this might lead to the stages of liking and conviction. These are more affective stages, focused on creating emotions like trust, which form the "contract" with the client. Ultimately, at the top of the hierarchy is the action stage. Action comes after the thresholds of cognition and emotion have been crossed. We could extend this behavioral portion of the model further to stages such as repurchase or loyalty, reflecting the dynamic nature of the relationship between an FA and a client.

This hierarchy of effects can form the basis for the objectives that an FA might set for a particular marketing communications effort. Whom are you trying to reach? Where are these people currently within the hierarchy? You should track this for each and every prospect. New prospects may need to be moved from the unaware to the awareness stage, and if so, an appropriate communications objective may simply be to create awareness among a percentage of the target market. Or, perhaps the FA will choose to focus on potential clients who are already aware and have a basic understanding of the FA's practice and specialties, but perhaps are not sure why this FA is specifically relevant to their needs.

So, the FA may set an objective of getting to know the client better in order to develop trust, empathy, a shared understanding of client needs, and an understanding of how she might be best able to help the client achieve his goals. Perhaps the FA is speaking with longtime clients who may be considering new products or increasing the percentage of overall assets invested with the FA. Again, the communication objectives would be different at this stage of the hierarchy, perhaps requiring the FA to overcome behavioral inertia on the part of the client. Not only are the objectives different at each level of the hierarchy, but the specific types of marketing communications channels and the messages themselves are likely to be different. Traditional advertising and PR may be best at creating awareness. Direct marketing and word of mouth may be better suited to establishing liking and conviction. Personal selling may be best at prompting action.

Coca-Cola, for example, has relied upon a strategy of "integrated proximity messaging," where the point is to deliver the right type of message for the right medium. The closer the consumer is to the point of sale, the more direct and immediate Coke becomes with its messages. For instance, the company delivers messages about how Coke fits with the consumer's life in its television advertising. In radio and billboard advertising, its messages ask or imply, "Aren't you thirsty now?" Outside the store, those messages might be even more direct, suggesting that Coca-Cola is available inside. And in the store, where action is most likely to occur, Coke might become very direct, suggesting that consumers refresh themselves *now*. Knowing whom you are talking to and his current mindset when you are talking to him are critical to the development of a strategy about both *what* to say and *where* (which media) to say it.

Consistent with our chapter on branding, all touchpoints between a brand and a client are opportunities for communication, and they all fall under the integrated marketing communications banner. For the rest of this chapter, however, we are going to focus on a smaller subset of communications options that FAs should be utilizing to their full potential: advertising, Web site design, and word of mouth. However, FAs using other types of communication vehicles should consider the same principles when putting together their promotions strategy.

ADVERTISING

There are many ways to create advertising messages: emotional messages, rational messages, ads that reflect a "slice of life," or ads that show a product demonstration. Regardless of the particular creative strategy, all advertisers should evaluate their ads with a few simple questions:

1. *Is the creative approach consistent with the brand's marketing and communication objectives?* Does it say what you want it to say about your brand? Is it consistent with an objective of raising awareness? Is it consistent with an objective of developing greater liking?
2. *Is the creative approach appropriate for the target audience?* Will the audience members understand it? Will it be persuasive? Does it reflect their concerns, objectives, or goals?
3. *Is the message of the ad clear and consistent?* Many ads are trying to say too many things at once and as a result end up communicating nothing at all.
4. *Does the ad reflect integration of all the other touchpoints between the brand and the target?*

In their tests regarding what makes advertising effective, Gallup and Robinson have identified some best practices.[3] First, they find that clearly indicating what the brand offers to the client is critical. How are you relevant to your clients' needs? These points of relevance must also be important to the client, and it must be believable that your brand can actually deliver on them. Beyond that, the brand needs to present itself in a compelling way. Ads are more compelling when the benefits of the brand are stated clearly and specifically and when the advertising message itself is simple. Furthermore, advertising is better at brand building when it clearly refers to the brand. We have all seen clever ads that make it difficult to figure out who is doing the advertising. Most clients won't spend the time to try to sort this out, and in general, you shouldn't ask them to work so hard to understand what you are trying to communicate or who is sending the message.

Another important set of decisions involves where to place the advertising message. First and foremost, this should be guided by an understanding of what media your target audience actually consumes. Will the audience members read, watch, listen to, or visit the media where your ad is placed? Will they notice the advertising once they are there? Despite every effort that you might make, most media alternatives will include many clients who are outside your target market.

Lastly, decisions about advertising should include some consideration regarding how to measure its effectiveness. While major advertisers can run large-scale tracking studies to get a sense of whether or not their advertising is working, most smaller advertisers don't have the resources to do this. As a result, tracking the influence of traditional advertising can be very difficult. Decide in advance how you will measure success and potential ROI.

WEB SITE DESIGN

A recent survey[4] clearly indicates the importance of an Internet presence for financial advisors. Overall, the survey found that affluent investors are Internet-savvy and use the Web for a variety of financial transactions. It found that 59 percent of affluent clients say that they rely on the Internet as their most important source of business information. Furthermore, 87 percent of them indicate that they use online banking services, and 64 percent say that they buy and sell stocks or other financial investments online. In addition, about two-fifths of these affluent investors spend more time on the Web than with other media, such as TV, radio, magazines, or newspapers. On average, affluent investors spend 18 hours a week on the Internet. Similarly, studies of financial advisors find that 93 percent agree that their clients want to access their accounts online, and 89 percent of advisors think their clients believe that they are better served if the FA uses technology. Another 67 percent agree that clients want to view their financial plans (not just their current positions) online.[5] These statistics speak to the relevance of the Internet as a communication channel for speaking with your clients.

Not every financial services firm allows its advisors to create their own personal Web sites. For those FAs who do have personal Web sites, the starting point of the design for the Web site, again, should be the FA's target market.

- To whom do you intend this Web site to speak?
- What are the objectives that you have for the Web site?

- What is the path by which you are differentiating yourself from your competitors (operational excellence, performance superiority, or customer intimacy, as described in Chapter 4)?

- Is your site meant to provide information about the array of products and services that you offer to potential new clients?

- Alternatively, perhaps your site can be a place where existing clients can come to learn about cutting-edge products and services. Perhaps you can provide links to podcasts and articles by leading analysts or educators about such cutting-edge products.

- Maybe your site is meant to be a portal that allows clients to access all their financial data in one convenient location. Perhaps you can provide password-protected access to the client's financial plan and links to the various client accounts that make up that plan.

In their 2003 report "Branding Financial Services on the Internet," authors Lindstrom and Anderson of Business Insights suggest answering the following questions:

- What do you want the clients to gain from your site *before* their visit (what might prompt them to make a visit to your Web site)?

- What do you want the clients to gain from your Web site *during* their visit?

- What do you want the clients to gain from your Web site *after* their visit?

We would add, what do you want your clients to know about your brand before, during, and after their visits to your Web site? What path are you choosing to differentiate yourself in providing value to your clients? How can you reflect that path through the content and design of your Web site? Your answers to these questions should guide your decisions about design and content.

It is also important to remember the mindset that clients bring with them to the Internet. Generally speaking, individuals who are on the Internet are goal-oriented and very directed. They are pursuing a particular outcome or experience, and they tend to do so with mental focus and little tolerance for distractions. When their experience with a Web site is seamless and interactive, clients find the process to be intrinsically enjoyable, and they achieve a sense of "flow."[6] While it sounds touchy-feely, this sense of flow is critical for Web site success and can help to promote return visits. An FA's Web site must be designed to take this into consideration.

You need to understand the goals that clients will bring to your Web site, not just your goals for what they should take away from it. You need to be sure that your design, layout, and content make it possible for them to achieve their goals quickly, efficiently, and with few interruptions, while at the same time meeting your branding objectives.

This can't be achieved without detailed knowledge of the actual experience that clients have when they are on your Web site. It requires a mechanism for feedback from clients, but also opportunities for the FA and the Web site designer to observe the client's actual experience to facilitate understanding of his objectives and to see where the Web site succeeds at delivering the necessary performance and where it fails. That is, rather than just looking at the number of clients that visit your site, make sure you measure which pages they visit, how long they stay there, what they click on, and so on. Can your clients get that sense of flow when they are interacting with your Web site? Sending your own team or staff members to test your Web site can be useful, but it isn't a replacement for testing with real clients who are trying to accomplish their actual goals.

WORD OF MOUTH

In our survey, we ask FAs to tell us the three most common ways by which prospective clients learn about their business. By far, the most frequent answer to that question is through referrals or word of mouth, either from other clients or from "centers of influence," such as lawyers and accountants. Word of mouth is mentioned more than three times as often as the next most common answers, which are seminars and direct personal contact from the FA. This isn't surprising.

Word of mouth is common and has tremendous impact on consumer decision making. There may be as many as 3.4 billion word-of-mouth conversations about products and services each day.[7] As many as 35 percent of Americans have conversations about financial services products or brands every day, with most of these conversations occurring face-to-face or via phone.[8] Unlike traditional marketing communications, word of mouth has tremendous credibility, even when it does not deserve it. When we see an ad, we know that the sponsor of that ad has a profit-making agenda behind the message. This agenda may or may not be consistent with our own personal interests. When someone we know recommends a product or service, we tend to pay attention. Generally, we don't think our friends or family members have a profit-making agenda when they tell us about a terrific new product or service. We tend to assume that if a friend passes along information about a service, it is because the service is genuinely good, and the friend thinks we would benefit from using it. The friend has our interests in mind.

Marketers have always known about the power of word of mouth, especially when it comes to the damage that negative word of mouth can do. With media fragmentation and message overload, word of mouth has gained new respect and has become a powerful tool for marketers. While in the past marketers were often content to hope that positive word of mouth for their brands would occur naturally [what the Word of Mouth Marketing Association (WOMMA) calls *organic* word of mouth], increasingly there is a realization among marketers that they can step in to seed, spark, and drive word of mouth (referred to by WOMMA as *amplified* word of mouth). We have asked FAs what specific actions, if any, they take to encourage or amplify word of mouth about their practice. While many FAs say that their most common tactic for encouraging word of mouth is simply to ask for it, a good number of respondents indicate that they do nothing at all. Given the importance of word of mouth in every FA's business, developing a strategy to encourage it and shape it is critical.

Not only should you be encouraging clients and collaborators to spread positive word of mouth about your practice, but you should also help them (and yourself) by making it easier for them to deliver that word of mouth to the right prospects and making sure that they are saying the right things in their conversations. Your clients and collaborators should know who your target segment is. You don't want them to spread word of mouth to just anyone. You want them to spread it to potential clients whom you can serve well and who will be valuable to you—potential clients in your target market.

Don't just ask for referrals. Ask for referrals to the right people. Make sure your clients know what characterizes your target market. This has several important benefits for you. First, it helps to ensure that the prospective clients who are coming your way really are good prospects for your business. Second, it prevents awkward situations in which you have to tell a potential referral, and indirectly the client or collaborator who provided the reference, that you really aren't the best person to serve her. Third, it reinforces your brand position in the mind of your existing clients. How do you do this? Tell your clients that you encourage them to tell others about what you have been able to help them do. Also, tell them that the clients you serve best are those who, like themselves, have certain characteristics. Be specific about those characteristics.

Once your clients know whom to talk to, make sure they know what to say. If they promise something that you can't deliver, they're probably not doing you any favors. You can't control what they say, but you can influence it. Make sure they know your three words (described in detail in Chapter 4). Make sure they know whether you are differentiating yourself through performance excellence or customer intimacy, for example. Make sure they can pass along your Web site address so that the prospective client can learn more for himself.

While you may want to encourage all of your existing clients to spread word of mouth, you may want to encourage it more from certain clients or collaborators than from others. Some people are naturally better at spreading word of mouth than others are. Take a look at your client list. Are there certain clients who have made more successful referrals in the past? Make sure you are encouraging future referrals from those clients. While you are at it, make sure you talk with those clients to try to get a better understanding of what makes them so good at referring. Is it because they know more of the right people? Is it because they are considered experts in this particular domain? Are they better communicators? Are they more satisfied and therefore say better things about your business? Outside that group, perhaps there are certain clients who are more likely to know other potential clients in your target market. Perhaps they're better connected in some way.

In their book *The Influentials*, authors Jon Berry and Ed Keller distill decades worth of research at Roper Polls into who spreads worth of mouth. In the book, they suggest that certain individuals are more likely to pass along word of mouth than others. These "influentials," for example, have a broader network of contacts, partly because they are more likely to be active in community associations and activities. Even in their leisure time, they are more likely to include other people in their plans, rather than engaging in activities alone or just with their immediate families. Importantly, it is not always the most affluent people who are the most influential. These influentials themselves might not be the most profitable clients based upon their own assets. But their value as providers of referrals could ultimately make them more valuable than clients with more investable assets (as discussed in Chapter 7).

WOMMA suggests a number of strategies to encourage positive word of mouth. Perhaps the most relevant is the suggestion that firms specifically encourage communications by developing tools that make it easier for clients to tell their friends, families, and colleagues about the firm. These tools could be as simple as making sure that your clients and collaborators know your target segment and your three words. Or they could be more developed. You might create materials specifically to be passed along as part of a word-of-mouth effort. Maybe you develop a special brochure or referral card that you leave with clients or collaborators that provides more details for prospects. In addition, WOMMA suggests making sure that people have something to talk about, such as information that could be shared or forwarded. People are more likely to talk when there is something new to say.

In their book *Made to Stick*, authors Chip and Dan Heath highlight results from their research on the aspects of messages that are especially likely to make them sticky. To make it more likely that a message will stick, the message should be (1) simple, (2) unexpected, (3) concrete, (4) credible, (5) emotional, and (6) part of a story or narrative. In addition, WOMMA suggests working within influential communities. These are people outside your client base who are likely to influence your target clients, such as accountants, lawyers, Realtors, bankers, and other centers of influence.

CONCLUSION

In the end, different FAs will use a different assortment of marketing communication methods to speak to current and potential clients. Whatever ways you ultimately choose, a few simple strategies can enhance the overall impact on your brand that these communication efforts will ultimately have. Marketing communications flow from your overall marketing strategy. Keep your marketing communications squarely focused on your clients. Don't make your messages about you; rather, make your messages about them and how you can be of help to them. Specify your objectives for each communication effort very clearly. Try to measure the outcome associated with each effort. Above all, make sure that all your efforts are integrated with one another and into the larger brand architecture that you are trying to build.

Make sure that you are speaking to your target market and saying the right things to position your brand as relevant to that market's needs. All of these efforts should be integrated with one another and with the broader set of touchpoints between your brand and your current or potential clients. Finally, make sure you articulate your goals for all communications efforts that you undertake very clearly and specifically so that you can really measure your success and implement changes going forward.

NOTES

1. Kevin Lane Keller, "Mastering the Marketing Communications Mix: Micro and Macro Perspectives on Integrated Marketing Communication Programs," *Journal of Marketing Management* 17 (2001), 819–847.

2. George Belch and Michael Belch, *Advertising and Promotion: An Integrated Marketing Communications Perspective* (New York: McGraw-Hill, 2009).

3. Scott C. Purvis and Philip Ward Burton, "It's the Benefit: Analysis of Which Ad Pulled Best? Examples Reveal How to Make Advertisements Pull Better," in *Which Ad Pulled Best?* (New York: McGraw-Hill, 2003).

4. Affluent Dynamics, "High-Net-Worth Investor study," sponsored by *Forbes*, January 2008.

5. Jaime Punishill with Ron Shevlin, Tom Watson, Steve Yonish, and Jeremy Sweeney, "Which Advisors Use Technology," Forrester Research, November 2002.

6. Thomas P. Novak, Donna L. Hoffman, and Adam Duhacek, "The Influence of Goal-Directed and Experiential Activities in Online Flow Experiences," *Journal of Consumer Psychology* 13, nos. 1 and 2 (2003), 3–17.

7. Ed Keller, Welcoming Remarks to the Word of Mouth Marketing Association Summit, Las Vegas, Nevada, November 14, 2007.

8. Keller Fay Group, "TalkTrack Survey Shows Banks Receive Twice the Word of Mouth of Other Financial Services," March 16, 2007.

CHAPTER 9

TACTICS AND BEST PRACTICES

Throughout the pages of this book, we have outlined strategies and tactics to help you build your business. Also, we have highlighted results from our survey of the more than 800 advisors we have taught in Wharton executive programs. In this chapter, we seek to delve deeper into the insights of the most successful advisors. We have combed our survey data and collected anecdotes from our interactions with financial advisors (FAs) to present you with the following best practices. Although the advice given here passes our scrutiny and is consistent with the frameworks we have built in the previous chapters, it is most definitely "direct from the horse's mouth."

Before we tell you about their insights, here is some information about the FAs who have come through our programs. For the most part, they are experienced, with

60 percent of them having been in the business for 10 years or more. Their teams manage large amounts of total assets: 46 percent have $500 million or more in assets under management, and another 30 percent have between $100 and $500 million. Also, 33 percent say that they individually serve fewer than 100 households, another 34 percent work with between 100 and 300 households, 24 percent work with 300 to 999 households, and 9 percent serve more than 1,000 households.

DIFFERENTIATING YOURSELF

Starting in Chapter 1, we emphasized the importance of differentiation. Clients clearly indicate that while trust and performance are important, they are not differentiating. Unfortunately, you cannot build a brand on nondifferentiating factors. So what should be the factors on which you differentiate? As we have said repeatedly, there must be a match-up between your strengths and the needs of your target segment. Furthermore, your points of differentiation must capture your value proposition and must be concise. This is why we advocate the three words test. You should be able to boil down your message to three words or less so that it is easily understood and conveyed by your word-of-mouth army.

A useful exercise to help you develop your message is to create an *elevator speech*. Certainly, the idea of cornering someone in an elevator with a high-pressure sales pitch is an antiquated notion and is probably not very effective. However, every FA should have a 15- to 30-second speech that clearly communicates his differentiating value proposition. Not only is this speech potentially useful in a number of situations, but the mere creation of it enables you to evaluate how easy it is to communicate your message. In our sessions, we often cold-call advisors and ask them, "Why should I invest with you?" Unfortunately, many FAs are wholly unprepared to answer this question. Many of them stumble and end up stringing together some awkward sentences using generic terms like *trust* and *performance*. If you are not immediately ready to communicate your message, how do you expect your clients to do it for you? Successful advisors are well practiced at this task and deliver a concise, differentiating, motivating, and effective message.

In preparation for our seminars, we ask advisors to imagine that they have 30 seconds with an attractive potential client and to list the reasons that this client should invest with them or their team. Here are some examples of great answers from highly successful advisors.

Advisor A:

- We are needs-based, focusing on goals and objectives.
- We work for the client, not our parent firm, per se.
- Our standards of service are elite.
- We are a resource.
- We educate you to provide you with the best possible advice.

This is a very good answer. You can see how the differentiating three words start to emerge: client-focused, independent, and resource/education-based.

Advisor B:

• We use a multigenerational approach.
• We give unbiased advice.
• We are not captive to any company's products.
• I won't get you the absolute highest investment results, but I'll make sure that you meet or exceed your financial goals.

Again, you can clearly see the points of differentiation: long-term multigenerational approach, independent, and unbiased. This answer has the additional merit of managing expectations. As we discussed in Chapter 5, expectations are a key driver of satisfaction. It is important to manage them from the first minute of the first interaction. This advisor clearly understands that assessing and managing expectations are essential to creating long-term client satisfaction and loyalty.

Advisor C:

• We take an educational approach rather than a sales approach.
• We are willing to take the time to continue to review and monitor a portfolio.
• We take the time to understand your needs.
• We take the time to explain investment options in detail.

This is one of our favorite answers. Perhaps the three words for this advisor are education, time, and control. This advisor knows that investors are often frustrated by not getting the time with their advisor that they need if they are to truly understand their investment options. Advisor C is trying to position himself against FAs who can't or won't take the time their clients need. Furthermore, these answers taken as a whole suggest a desire to appeal to clients' underlying need for control. As we discussed in Chapter 5, advisors often inadvertently rob clients of their sense of control. This advisor wants to bolster that need for control through education and by taking the time to fully review and monitor investments and strategies.

Advisor D:

- We have a proven track record over 25 years (experience).
- We have a dedicated team of specialists (efficiency).
- We engage in ongoing training and maintaining our credentials (expertise).
- We have local expertise with global resources (we are a local firm with global resources through our partnering with our parent firm).

This advisor is evidently on the same page as we are. The three words (experience, efficiency, and expertise) are right there in the answer. Moreover, Advisor D also implies independence by casting her parent firm as a collaborator whose resources can be leveraged only when needed.

GETTING REFERRALS

As previously discussed, by far the most common way in which new prospects learn about an FA is through word of mouth, either from a client or from another trusted advisor. When we ask advisors what specific tactics they use to encourage word of mouth, many FAs tell us that they do nothing at all. Given that referrals drive your business, a passive strategy is obviously inadequate. Others simply say something like, "Provide good service so that our clients will want to tell others about us." This is absolutely something that advisors should be doing, but this passive approach seems to be based on hope. Hope is not an effective marketing tactic.

As simple as it sounds, the best advisors agree that you must proactively ask for referrals. One FA said, "Ask your current clients. Include a line about referrals in all your letters to clients." Another said, "I explicitly volunteer to help friends and families of my existing clients." More direct and focused is still another FA, who said, "I remind my ideal clients that I want people just like them. Ask them to suggest people who they know through work, their social clubs, and so on." This advisor is explicitly taking control of word of mouth in her business. She is asking her best clients to help her identify people just like them. Another FA goes beyond this to make sure that her best clients also know what to say when they spread word of mouth about her: "We identify our ideal clients, educate them on our process and philosophy, and make them our advocates." Given its importance to every advisor's business, word of mouth is too important to approach passively and just hope it works out for the best.

If you are truly providing good value to your clients, they will want to recommend you. Satisfied clients who are loyal have a vested interest in your success and will want to bring you clients. However, some people are naturally more inclined than others to actually do this. By asking them, you are not only priming them to do so, but also giving them permission. When clients make solid recommendations to their friends and family, they are doing them a favor.

Lastly, FAs emphasize the importance of following up on referrals, both with the client and with the prospect. After receiving permission to contact a prospect, you must reach out in a timely manner. Failure to do so could send a message to your client that his referrals are not important to you. You also want to reinforce your clients for referring prospects to you, so many FAs send thank-you notes for recommendations. In addition, and this relates to Chapter 7 and customer lifetime value, keep track of your interactions with all potential clients. This can be your "ROI calculator" that can give you information about a particular individual client, such as how much effort it took to obtain her business in terms of number of contacts and amount of time. It also provides you with information on where you might need to improve your business. For instance, are you not good at closing the deal because it takes on average nine interactions and only 20 percent of your prospects become clients?

LEARNING ABOUT PROSPECTS

We have also asked questions to better understand what kinds of data FAs collect about potential clients. In one question, we asked, "Imagine an individual you are trying to attract as a client. What are the three most important pieces of information you would want to know that you believe would help maximize your chances of getting their business?" The most common answers are

- Their financial goals.
- Their financial concerns.
- Information about their family situation.
- What is important to them? What do they care about?
- What is their risk profile?

These are all useful pieces of information, but consider some of the responses that we get less frequently, such as

- What common contacts, friends, or centers of influence do we share?
- Which of our clients do they already know, and which do they know best?
- Do they have interests in philanthropy?
- What are their values?
- What are their passions? What gets them out of bed in the morning?
- Who is their current/past advisor, and what do they like best and least about that advisor?
- If we could meet five years from today, with everything in your life having worked perfectly, describe what that situation would be.
- Beyond financial issues, what is most important to them about the rest of their lives?

Answers to these latter questions might frame and provide context for the answers given to the first set of questions, providing deeper insight into *why* a particular client might have certain financial goals and what her decision-making process is. Understanding why certain goals are important to a prospect might be more meaningful than just knowing that these goals exist.

We have found that successful advisors have a well-scripted *question protocol* for initial meetings with new and prospective clients. They know what questions to ask and how to assess the answers. They try to understand the clients' needs and decision-making process, determine if there is a good fit, and begin to calibrate and manage expectations during the first meeting.

LEARNING ABOUT YOUR CLIENTS: ESTABLISH A BOARD OF ADVISORS

Understanding your customers is a bedrock principle of business. One of the most important pieces of advice we have heard in our work with FAs is to establish a *board of advisors*. We have never spoken to an advisor who did not think that this was a worthwhile exercise once he had done it. Although the boards vary in composition, they are most commonly made up of a small number of current clients. Most meet two to four times a year to discuss what they think of the FA's work and the FA's team, their broader financial concerns or issues, and how the FA could better address those concerns or issues. Sometimes the FA will ask these advisors to serve in the role for an "official" length of time, such as a year or two. Other times, the FA institutes a series of meetings, with the exact membership of the board of advisors rotating from meeting to meeting.

Many advisors wonder how you get busy people to commit to doing this, but the FAs who have done it say that it is easier than it sounds. You have to carefully choose which clients to ask, and you have to ask them the right way. Let them know that this will not be a selling opportunity for you, but rather an opportunity for you to learn from them. Clients generally appreciate the chance to give feedback that will lead to improvements in the service that they receive. Tell them that you want to hear the good and the bad on all issues, no matter how big or how small. You may get some information that surprises you, but you have to make sure that you really listen. Several FAs have told us that their first few meetings were pretty painful, as they heard all the ways in which their clients thought they could be delivering better service. Criticism, even when politely phrased, can be hard to take. All have said, however, that this criticism was eye-opening. Often they had no idea what issues their clients were unhappy with. The insights genuinely helped them to serve their clients better. Beyond feedback about how you are serving your clients, these boards can help you keep track of trends, issues, and opportunities to which your clients are responding. The board members can talk about their own social networks and give you deeper insight into your target market.

Other FAs have mentioned having a more informal board of potential collaborators or influencers that they meet frequently for breakfast or lunch. This group shares insights about trends and issues that might affect clients and brainstorms solutions that they can enact separately or together.

Again, this is an opportunity to gain deeper and timelier insights into the decisions and issues that your target market finds itself facing.

Overall, a board of advisors can be an effective alternative way to collect data. You can collect data on how your clients view you, your brand, and the services you provide. For example, ask your clients what thoughts or associations come to mind when they think of your brand. What three words would they use to describe you? Do they come up with the associations or the three words that you have in mind?

Often you don't need to collect reams of quantitative data to get the insights you need. Frequently, the issue is getting past the day-to-day tasks you face to really understand how your service fits into your clients' life. For example, when Procter & Gamble (P&G) recently wanted to expand its business among professional clients, rather than end user consumers, it sent out teams of researchers to observe how janitors, fast-food workers, maids, and launderers carried out their jobs. P&G managers even helped clean the rooms at some hotels in order to learn what worked and what didn't. For example, observing workers at the fast-food chain Wendy's revealed that employee turnover and the resulting need to train new employees on cleaning techniques was a major headache for clients. P&G decided to offer customized videos and laminated guides for workers on how to clean different parts of the restaurant properly. Cleaning supplies and tools were color-coded according to product and task to supplement the training function and resolve a customer's need.

Simple observations of what was working and what was not working in the real world led to innovations in how P&G served its clients. You may not be able to hang out in your clients' homes and observe how they make financial decisions, but simple innovations like a board of advisors can give you insights that you might not otherwise get through your regular meetings with clients.

One last opportunity we have heard about regarding a board of advisors is to form a network of nonthreatening FAs who can act as a sounding board. This is not meant to replace the board made up of your clients, but to supplement it. That is, imagine that you ask three or four other advisors who impress you at conferences that you attend to serve on your board and, of course, offer to do the same for them. You can then share best practices and discuss what is working and what is not from the FA's perspective. Our 700+ FAs have suggested that they not only would welcome this, but would use it often.

If what we have said already is not enough to drive home the need for a board of advisors, literally at the time of writing this book, the government has approved a $700 billion financial bailout package that will probably be part of financial history by the time you are reading this. Who among us could possibly say that her clients are not concerned, or at least uncertain, and wouldn't welcome an opportunity to talk about it? Don't wait for their concerns to bubble to you. Be proactive and ask them.

BUILDING AFFINITY

When we asked advisors about their best practices with respect to building client relationships, many of the FAs in our survey have put "client appreciation events and seminars" at the top of the list. From speaking with FAs in our class sessions, we have found that these events range from very casual ones, such as an evening of dinner and drinks at the FA's home, to much more formal affairs, such as educational events on economic and financial topics. These events offer an opportunity to bring clients together in a group setting that isn't focused on selling.

Many FAs hold such events, but the most savvy have offered some valuable words of advice about how to leverage these events to the fullest. For instance:

- Choose whom you invite.
- Put your guest list together carefully.

If you set things up so that you create opportunities for your clients to network with one another, you will increase the value of these events to them. Not only might they learn something and get to know your brand better, but they also might have the opportunity to further their own personal or professional interests at the same time.

- Organize the event well.
- Make it worth attending.

If your clients know that your events will be engaging, educational, or just plain fun, they are much more likely to accept your invitation. If they've attended an event that was awkward, poorly organized, or boring, they're never going to come back, and they are likely to tell your other clients not to attend in the future. Specialized, as opposed to general, topics that you know match up with particular clients' needs work best.

- Don't plan an event or invite clients at the last minute.
- Take advantage of precommitment effects and send your invitation early.

As we discussed in Chapter 6, clients are more likely to agree to do something when it is off in the future than when it is tomorrow. Take advantage of this inertia effect and send out your invitations early enough to secure clients' commitment to attend while their calendars are still relatively empty.

One FA told us about a very successful event he had done several times for his clients and their young adult children. The advisor had invited clients to bring their children who had just gotten married or were about to have their first child. The focus of the seminar was on the implications of these life changes and how financial and other plans need to be changed or updated. At these events, the FA covered a wide range of topics that were financially relevant, but not necessarily investment related. He invited some of his current clients to look back and talk about their best decisions and discuss things they wish they had done differently when they were at the same point in their lives. This particular FA is focused on growing his business by managing generations of wealth, and these seminars are perfectly targeted to meet that objective.

Another top response for building affinity is to be visible in the "community and local charities." We can't emphasize enough the importance of community activity. It helps to accomplish many goals at the same time. First, it helps to create awareness for your brand. While it might require a substantial investment of time, it requires less financial investment than many other ways of obtaining the same reach. Also, community involvement naturally provides opportunities to network and to get to know potential clients. As we discussed in Chapter 8, those who are most involved in their communities are also the most likely to spread word of mouth. That is, these people are the "influentials." By participating in community endeavors with them, you make it more likely that this valuable group knows you and can tell others about you. Furthermore, your participation in activities that are meaningful to your clients helps you to have a better understanding of their motivations and to better position yourself as truly relevant to them.

In one of our sessions here at Wharton, an FA described a charity golf tournament that he organizes annually. Each year, he asks one of his best clients to "host" the event, choosing the charity organization that will benefit and suggesting potential invitees. The FA's office then organizes the event. He spoke about how much these clients value the opportunity to lead such an effort to benefit their chosen charity—so much so that several clients have already asked to be the designated host for the tournament in future years. The people that the hosts invite to participate are often other community leaders, giving the FA an opportunity to get to know them better, and also giving all the attendees an opportunity to network. In addition, the FA invites a group of his top clients, select prospective clients, and a small group of local accountants and lawyers who are important centers of influence. He organizes the groups that golf together, facilitating opportunities for people with similar interests to get to know one another and giving key clients an opportunity to make recommendations. Most years, he said, the tournament has led to local press coverage.

Other FAs have told us that they make sure that they or members of their team are on the boards of local organizations, acting as community leaders and getting involved with current and potential clients who care about local issues. Another told us about serving as a guest speaker at local investment clubs, a particularly important audience for her, as her target market is high-net-worth women. Nearly every month for the past year, she has spoken to local clubs, gaining several new clients and referrals. Moreover, she has boosted her credentials as a knowledgeable, trustworthy, and objective advisor for women. This example also reinforces the importance of choosing to be active in a way that reinforces the way you want your brand to be perceived by others.

In our survey and in our classroom sessions, we also ask advisors to share their best advice for *building relationships*. Here are some of their words of wisdom:

- Don't talk primarily about money—find out what else drives them. What is their passion? What is their business? What do they enjoy? What are their goals (short and long term)?

  Certainly clients are interested in their financial well-being, but it isn't the only thing they are interested in. Most clients expect financial performance, but it is not the primary reason that they choose a particular FA. They take it for granted that an advisor will promise performance. Moreover, their financial status and investment performance are really the means to some end that they have in mind. This FA suggests that you focus on the larger goal, rather than focusing on the means to that end. Your clients' goals, passions, and interests are the real reasons they care about their financial situation. Make yourself relevant to those bigger goals, and you will be on the path to forming long-lasting relationships with your clients.

- Don't tell them how you can help them. Ask them how you can help them! There is no more powerful question than, "What is important to you?"

This is the essence of being client-focused rather than focused on yourself. Your ability to serve your clients starts with an understanding of what they want. Start with them.

- Get client buy-in (partnering) on an idea, strategy, or plan, and use *we* when you are successful—this will engender positive feelings and build the relationship. When an investment strategy isn't working, use *I*, and never be afraid to apologize.

These are the basics of relationship building, whether within the interpersonal domain or in business. Build your partnership on a shared foundation of goals and objectives. Share the credit for the success in your endeavors. Take responsibility when something goes wrong, and create a plan together to overcome the current difficulties.

CONCLUSION

This chapter is all about learning from some of the most successful advisors. These FAs have provided some great advice and effective tactics. However, keep in mind that simply replicating one or two of these ideas in isolation is not enough. You must view tactics like question protocols, client events, and community involvement as parts of a broader client development and brand-building strategy. In other words, your tactics should be carefully chosen and integrated. They should fit with your strengths and flow comfortably from your carefully designed strategy.

CHAPTER 10

PUTTING IT ALL TOGETHER: YOUR MARKETING PLAN

If you have gotten this far in the book, it is likely that you are serious about taking a service-oriented, client-centric approach to your financial advising practice. As an entrepreneur, you understand that the effort you put into marketing is an investment to grow your business for the long term. In the previous chapters, we have delved into important issues like managing your brand, finding your niche, understanding your clients and their psychology, managing client value, and creating your integrated marketing communications campaign. Putting thought into these issues is important, but creating a plan for action is vital. Many studies have shown that without a written plan, even if it is just a sketch or outline as we describe here, you are much less likely to achieve your goals. This is the chapter that will help you bring together all of the pieces in a concise and actionable marketing plan. In our survey, only 58 percent of FAs had a marketing plan. Of those with a plan, just 65 percent had updated it within the last year. This clearly represents a lost opportunity for many advisors.

Why is it necessary to create a marketing plan? Simply put, it is a resource for you, your partners, and your staff to guide your business into the future. You must have a clear statement of who you are, what you stand for, whom you serve, and why clients should invest with you. Putting this information into a concise, accessible document will help to focus your efforts, as well as those of your partners and your staff. If you expect your clients to tell others why they invest with you, then you should have a clear idea yourself.

Why would you choose *not* to create a plan? Perhaps you feel that doing so will be too time-consuming. We have acknowledged throughout the book that the up-front investment in marketing will not necessarily have a short-term payoff. However, we have argued that marketing is just that: an investment. It is an investment in the long-term success of your practice. This perspective is the key difference between a short-term, sales-oriented focus and an entrepreneurial, long-run, business-building orientation. By reading this book, you have made much of the investment already. Don't waste it.

Similarly, you might feel that your practice is doing very well without a marketing focus, so why should you make the effort when you are already successful? This perspective is short-sighted and dangerous to the future of your business. Unfortunately, it is a mistake that is all too common, and it is called the "liability of success." The road is littered with the carcasses of businesses that had great success early, but collapsed when the environment changed. These failed businesses took an "if it ain't broke, don't fix it" approach to business. If you don't invest in understanding your business and your clients today, you will not be prepared to react when things inevitably change. At the time of the writing of this book, Congress has just approved an $800+ billion bailout package to address the deepest global financial crisis since the Great Depression. This is certainly a radical environmental change.

Chapter 1 created the structure for a strategic marketing plan, and throughout the book we have taken you through specific theories, frameworks, and analyses. All of this ends where we began: with the five Cs, STP, and the four Ps (see Figure 10.1). You must understand your *clients'* needs and decision-making processes. You must strategically analyze the strengths and weaknesses of your *company* (which is you!). You must know your *competition*. You must understand the broader *context* and leverage your *collaborators*. Next, you need to specialize by *segmenting* your customer base and *positioning* yourself to serve a specific *target* group of clients. Lastly, you must formulate an integrated marketing mix that offers the right set of *products* that are *placed* (delivered), *priced*, and *promoted* in the most appropriate way.

Figure 10.1 Broad Outline of Marketing Plan

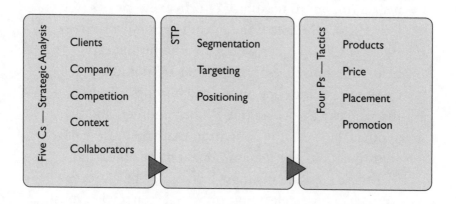

We recognize that this is a huge task that could result in a voluminous document. Creating a huge marketing dissertation (or, more likely, a paperweight) for your business is not the goal here. Pragmatism dictates that you create a very concise tool that will help everyone who is involved in your business to focus on the right things. Also, make your plan accessible and easily updatable. Ask others to help contribute to it; when people contribute to the creation of a plan, they are much more likely to adhere to its principles.

Thus, we offer first a set of broad recommendations that flow directly from the previous chapters. Second, we suggest creating a positioning statement to bring together some of the key insights. Lastly, we offer a template for a one-page marketing plan that will be useful to you and everyone involved with your business.

BROAD RECOMMENDATIONS

1. *Strategy should inform tactics.* Many advisors and large firms alike believe that tactical changes are the key to success. Tactics can move the needle in the near term, but to maximize effectiveness, tactics (the four Ps) should flow from a firmly grounded strategy (the five Cs). In other words, do not put the cart before the horse. Also, tactics that are not integrated can interfere with one another. This does not mean that you can't work on one P, then another, and then another. However, it does mean that you must make adjustments in one P conditional on the others and that these adjustments must be directed by a broader strategy. Thus, a clear and informed strategy is a must.

2. *Know your brand, and know that you are a brand.* One of your most important assets is your reputation. You must treat it like a brand. You must invest in it, protect it, cultivate it, and leverage it.

3. *Understand your value proposition and points of differentiation.* If you can't communicate clearly and concisely why someone should invest with you, how can you expect your clients to do it for you? This should be boiled down to your three words.

4. *Be consistent.* Everything in your practice should reinforce the brand that you are trying to build. Inventory and integrate all of your touchpoints and center your message around your three words.

5. *Specialize.* Identify your niche by matching your strengths, relative to those of your competition, to a specific target group of clients. Gear your strategy to serve this niche better than anyone else.

6. *Research and understand your clients.* Along with your brand, your clients are your most valuable asset. Invest time and effort in understanding them and better serving them.

7. *Make relationship building routine.* Client lifetime value (CLV) is the key driver of long-term profitability. You must actively manage your relationships with your clients to maximize CLV.

8. *Create your word-of-mouth army.* You know that referrals drive your business, but they don't just happen. You must provide superior value, encourage your clients to refer you, and leverage collaborative centers of influence.

YOUR POSITIONING STATEMENT

A positioning statement is a critical tool for your marketing strategy. It refines your strategy, informs your tactics, and clarifies your communications. It is an invaluable tool for your business and your clients. However, a positioning statement is not a tagline. While it can be used as the basis for creating external communications, its primary purpose is to bring together multiple elements of your marketing strategy into a concise and comparative statement.

An effective positioning statement needs to answer the following questions:

- Who are you?
- What business are you in?
- Whom do you serve (target clients)?
- What do the target clients whom you serve need?
- Who is your competition?
- What is your key benefit/point of differentiation?
- Why should a target client believe you?

Positioning statements come in many forms, but we suggest the following:

(Company, Brand, Person)
is the **(business you are in)**
that provides **(the target client)**
with **(key benefit/point of differentiation)**
unlike **(competition)**
because **(reason clients should believe you can deliver the benefit/point of differentiation)**.

A positioning statement should be evaluated by the following criteria:

- Does it motivate the client or prospect?
- Does it differentiate you from the competition?
- Is it unique?
- Is it credible and believable?

For example, a mock positioning statement might be:

Jane Smith Advisors

is the wealth management firm

that provides nearly retired individuals

with unique long-term health, financial, and estate-planning ideas

unlike larger firms

because of our full-service, individualized approach to your family's needs.

MARKETING PLAN

Your marketing plan should be concise and actionable. It should be motivating to you and your current staff and can serve as a primer for new staff members. Furthermore, it should be something that you can easily refer to and update. While your one-page marketing plan can take different forms, it should at a minimum include the elements listed here. Beneath each element, in italics, we give a brief example. This example is not meant to be the right marketing plan for you; it is a sample one that contains an integrated set of statements for a hypothetical practice.

- Statement of purpose

  To become the best and most trusted "socially responsible" financial services practice

- Situational and contextual framework

  in our community, which is very socially and environmentally conscious.

- Point of differentiation—your three words

  Philanthropy, social impact, globally oriented.

- Primary target niche

  Individuals with a desire to do good and give back with their wealth.

- Secondary target niche

  Nearly retired clients who are looking for the next impact and challenge.

- Key client (referral) list, both financial and strategic

  Amy Hopkins, local environmental group president
  David Smith, environmental attorney
  Jane Thompson, accountant
  Ronald Jones, civic leader

Dr. Mary Williams, physician who does extensive pro bono work

- Competitive set

ABC Advisors, which targets the philanthropic, pro-environment, and near-retirement segment.

- Tactics
  - ○ Product: core and differentiating offerings

A complete list of appropriate philanthropic causes and socially responsible and green investments.

  - ○ Place: service delivery model

A work environment that emphasizes "green." Appropriate colors, solar lighting, lots of plants, recycling opportunities, and so on.

  - ○ Price: fee and commission structure

We charge a flat percentage fee of X and donate a fraction of our commissions to the following local and global charities.

  - ○ Promotion: communication standards and media

The goal is to generate a PR army by getting referrals from established environmentally friendly firms, the press, and local community groups. List local publications (or sections of local publications) that target clients are likely to read. List local events that they are likely to attend.

○ Control: key metrics for tracking progress and growth

Clients who mention "green" and socially responsible investing. Fraction of clients' investments in environmentally related and socially responsible industries. Commissions delivered to charities. Mentions in newspapers and other media. Average client lifetime value and net present value of clients.

FINAL ADVICE

A marketing plan is as much about attitude as it is about strategy and tactics. No great advisor wakes up in the morning and says to himself, "Damn, I have to interact with people again," or, "Damn, I have to learn about my clients' needs today." For your marketing plan to be effective, you must truly believe that your investment will pay off.

Start by implementing many of the suggestions in this book, and we assert that one or all of three things will happen:

1. You will grow your business because of the client-centric approach that you have taken.
2. You will enjoy the clients you have more because they will better match your skills and capabilities.
3. It will take you less time to do the same amount of business (potentially improving your quality of life) because you now have a strategy for working effectively with your clients.

We would say, "Good luck," but taking a marketing-oriented approach will be your best chance to welcome luck your way.

EXPANDED SURVEY RESULTS

We have surveyed more than 800 financial advisors who have attended executive education programs here at the Wharton School. These advisors are among the most successful in the business and work for a number of the largest financial services firms in the United States. Each time a group comes to Wharton, we ask each participant to complete a short survey about his current marketing practices. Not everyone takes the time to complete the survey, but most do. Many of the survey results are discussed throughout the various chapters of this book. In this appendix, we provide you with a more complete look at the responses. It leads, of course, to the provocative question:

How do you stack up against the competition?

Figures A.1 to A.3 provide some basic information on our survey respondents. In general, they are very experienced. A full 61 percent have been in the industry for at least 10 years, and a quarter of them have more than 20 years of

Figure A.1 How Long Have You Been a Financial Professional?

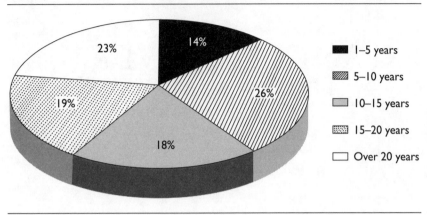

- 1–5 years
- 5–10 years
- 10–15 years
- 15–20 years
- Over 20 years

Figure A.2 What Is the Total Amount of Assets That Your Financial Professional Team Has Under Management?

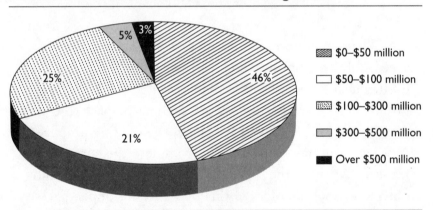

- $0–$50 million
- $50–$100 million
- $100–$300 million
- $300–$500 million
- Over $500 million

experience as financial advisors. Only 14 percent have fewer than five years of experience. Nearly half of them (46 percent) manage $50 million or less in total assets with their teams, though another 46 percent manage between $50 and $300 million in assets. Importantly, about 50 percent of the respondents' teams work with fewer than 300 total client

Figure A.3 How Many Client Households Does Your Financial Professional Team Serve?

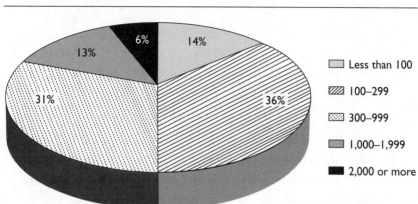

households. Another 31 percent say that their team works with between 300 and 999 client households but that they individually work with fewer clients. Most teams are working with between 300 and 500 client households.

This is important because when we offer advice about focusing on a target segment, financial advisors often will express concern that this will be too limiting and will prevent them from achieving the critical mass of clients they need to serve. However, if the vast majority of financial advisor practices can serve at most 500 client households, they don't need to target segments of potential clients that number in the many hundreds or even thousands. A narrower, more focused target will be more than sufficient to achieve an appropriate client base and assets under management.

Figure A.4 shows that just over 41 percent of our survey respondents indicate that they have not prepared a comprehensive marketing plan for their practice. That's 41 percent! We suspect that in the broader marketplace, the percentage who have not created a marketing plan is even higher, as our respondents represent some of the most successful advisors in the industry and tend to have extensive experience.

All advisors are looking to grow their businesses and to better serve their clients. From our perspective, taking the time to create a marketing plan is "low-hanging fruit." There are many steps you could take to improve your business, but few are likely to be as simple or to yield as many benefits as taking the time to put together a marketing plan. Furthermore, your marketing plan will provide the road map by which you will discover other low-hanging fruit opportunities.

Why would you choose *not* to create a plan? Perhaps you feel that doing so will be too time-consuming. We have acknowledged throughout the book that the up-front investment in marketing will not necessarily have a short-term payoff. However, we have argued that marketing is just that: an investment. It is an investment in the long-term

Figure A.4 Do You Have a Comprehensive Marketing Plan for Your Practice?

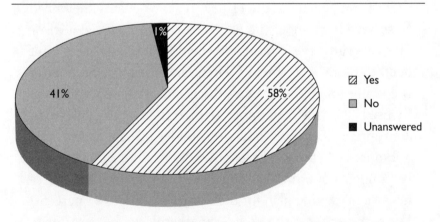

success of your practice. This perspective is the key difference between a short-term, sales-oriented focus and an
entrepreneurial, long-run, business-building orientation. By
reading this book, you have made much of the investment
already. Don't waste it.

Chapter 1 of this book lays out the structure for a strategic marketing plan, and throughout the book we take you
through specific theories, frameworks, and analyses. All of
this ends where we began: with the five Cs, STP, and the
four Ps. You must understand your *clients'* needs and decision-making processes. You must strategically analyze the
strengths and weaknesses of your *company* (which is you!).
You must know your *competition*. You must understand the
broader *context* and leverage your *collaborators*. Next, you
need to specialize by *segmenting* your customer base and
positioning yourself to serve a specific *target* group of clients.
Lastly, you must formulate an integrated marketing mix
that offers the right set of *products* that are *placed* (delivered),
priced, and *promoted* in the most appropriate way.

Of those who answered yes to the previous question ("Do
you have a comprehensive marketing plan?"), we further
asked when that marketing plan was written. As you can see
from Figure A.5, the majority of respondents indicated that
their marketing plan was less than a year old at the time they
answered the survey. However, 35 percent of respondents
clearly have an outdated marketing plan, written more than
a year ago. Those whose marketing plans are more than
three years old are really behind.

A marketing plan is something that should be updated
on a yearly basis. Why? Because the market changes. If you
wrote your marketing plan in the middle of 2007, it will

Figure A.5 If You Do Have a Comprehensive Marketing Plan, When Was It Written?

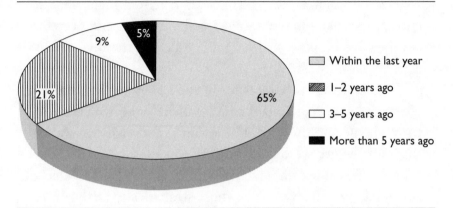

Within the last year

1–2 years ago

3–5 years ago

More than 5 years ago

clearly be outdated by the middle of 2009. The *context* has changed as a result of economic trends, and no doubt your *competitive* landscape has changed as a result of the major upheaval in the industry. The mindsets of your *clients* have probably changed—they are likely to be more anxious. Their investable assets have probably declined substantially, adding to that anxiety! Your *company*'s strengths and weaknesses (your strengths and weaknesses) may have changed as well. Similarly, you may need to take advantage of different skill sets possessed by *collaborators*. Or perhaps some of those collaborators have moved into the role of competitors in some way. Even if you wish to continue to serve the same target segment of clients, you may need to change the *products* you offer them or make adjustments to your *pricing, promotion,* or *place* strategy because of the changes that you have noted in your five Cs analysis. As discussed in the preface to this book, these "rough seas" are a time to reevaluate your marketing plan and to become more efficient than ever!

Figure A.6 Do You and/or Your Financial Professional Team Have a Target Segment on Which You Focus?

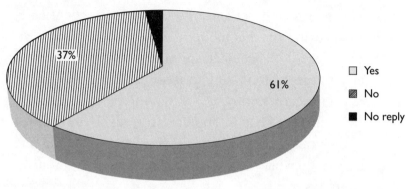

While 61 percent of our respondents indicate that they do have a target segment on which they focus (see Figure A.6), nearly 40 percent do not. Chapters 2 and 3 discuss the importance of segmentation for a financial advisor's (FA's) practice. Simply put, segmentation involves recognizing that different clients want different things and that not all clients share the same underlying preferences for the products and/or services that an FA might offer. Because different segments want different things, they will feel better served, and more satisfied, if you can give them exactly what they want and nothing else. Given a broad assortment of preferences for different types of service and products, an FA will want to carefully choose which segments she wishes to focus on, and hopefully after reading this book you determine that using the methods of Chapter 7 will provide you a quantitative way to think about it.

One of the (false) arguments against segmentation that is commonly made is that it restricts an advisor to a small fraction of potential clients. For example, imagine that in your local area, you decide to focus on high-net-worth lawyers, who represent 3 percent of your potential client base. Doesn't focusing on this niche market restrict your business potential? We argue just the opposite—segmentation is exactly the right long-run strategy, and your ability to acquire significant numbers of customers happens segment by segment. That is, you are more likely to succeed in attracting and retaining clients if you focus on giving one segment exactly what it wants. In contrast, the FA who tries to be all things to all potential clients may not be giving *any* individual client what he wants and ultimately becomes less attractive to everyone.

Chapter 2 makes it clear that we believe that a segmentation strategy is critical to long-term success. The diversity of clients and the seemingly infinite variety of investment vehicles that is available make being a true generalist nearly impossible. How can you believably be the expert on helping newly retired individuals create a long-term income plan while also being the go-to advisor for wealthy young entrepreneurs? Moreover, managing wealth has become more complex, as clients are seeking out an ever-expanding variety of investment vehicles. Beyond traditional plans that involve equities, fixed income, and cash, investors are increasingly becoming interested in REITs, commercial and investment real estate, commodities, private equity, hedge funds, foreign currency, socially responsible investing, green investing, and so on. Add in the tax implications, and it is more than one individual advisor can hope to do well. The answer is to specialize. Either individually or within a team practice (i.e., a group of specialists), you must identify a segment that matches your strengths and tailor a marketing mix to that segment. We strongly believe that advisors with a clear target segment are at an advantage over advisors who pursue anybody and everybody who wants to invest with them.

While we are pleased to see that 61 percent of our respondents indicate that they do have a target segment that they focus on, when we dig a little deeper to find out more details about that target segment, we often find that it is a very generic one. The most common segments identified in our survey were high-net-worth (HNW) individuals, the at-retirement market, and small business owners. While classifying clients as HNW and at-retirement narrows down the market somewhat, we consider these to be sectors that have more refined segments or niches within them. Do all HNW investors want the same things? Probably not. There are subsegments within the HNW (and other) segment. In addition to small business owners, advisors identified more narrow niches, such as nonprofit organizations and employees, particular school district employees, employees and executives of individual companies, specific ethnic groups, and specific groups of professionals. Chapter 3 breaks down these segments and niches even further and offers guidance on how to think more strategically about identifying them and serving them.

The question in Figure A.7 is aimed at understanding how FAs figure out whether or not a potential client is in their target segment. Certainly understanding a prospective client's current financial situation is important, and it may help an FA to determine whether or not a prospective client has adequate assets, for example, to be a part of the target market. But information about a client's current financial situation may not tell you much about the client's actual

Figure A.7 Imagine a High-Net-Worth Individual That You Are Trying to Attract as a Client. What Are the Three Most Important Pieces of Information You Would Want to Know That You Believe Would Help Maximize Your Chances of Getting This Person's Business?

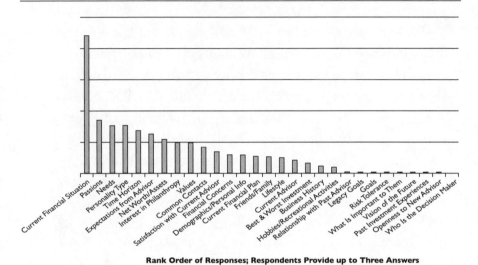

Rank Order of Responses; Respondents Provide up to Three Answers

need states. In Chapter 4, we lay out a number of different types of needs or motivational states that may drive a client's purchases of financial services—needs like self-actualization, need for control, and need for esteem. Questions that try to assess these deeper needs and mindsets toward financial services are likely to better help you speak directly to that specific client. That is, motivational states (e.g., need for control) tend to be all-encompassing and permeate to wants and needs for all products and services. Thus, the more you can probe beyond demographic and asset-based questions to get at underlying needs, the more you can speak to that client about the value of a potential relationship with you rather than with another advisor. Ask questions that tell

Figure A.8 What Percentage of Your Business Is in the "At-Retirement" Stage?

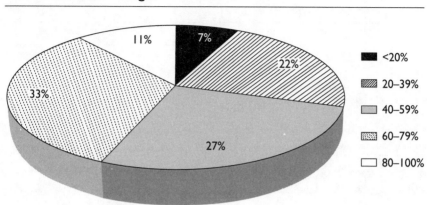

you what you need to do to serve this client or determine if someone else could serve her better.

A clear trend in the financial services industry is a focus on baby boomers and retirement (see Figure A.8). Many of the participants in our programs at Wharton are focused on this segment. While asking your clients questions that can help you infer their motivational state (as just mentioned) is valuable, it is important to identify those who are in an "at-retirement" mindset. It is likely that these clients are concerned with wealth preservation and are feeling particularly threatened by the current economic crisis.

The question in Figure A.9 asks financial advisors to make themselves relevant to potential clients and to differentiate themselves from their competitors. In 30 seconds, can you explain your unique value proposition to a prospective client? What makes you relevant to his needs? What makes you more relevant than your competitors? Unfortunately,

**Figure A.9 Imagine You Are Stuck in an Elevator for 30 Seconds
with a Potential HNW Client. What Are Five Reasons
That He Should Invest with You?**

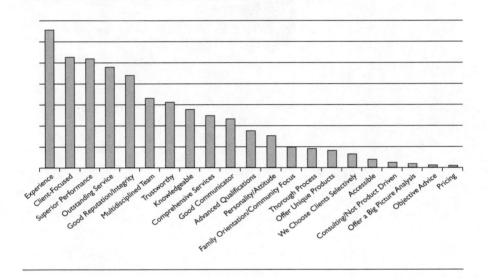

what we find over and over again is that the vast majority of
FAs say the same things about themselves. Take a look at
the top five reasons on the chart. Most FAs say that they are
experienced and client focused, offer superior performance
and outstanding service, and have a good reputation and
integrity. These are all worthy attributes to have, but nearly
everyone is claiming them. Everyone is positioning herself
in the same way.

Our data and discussions with FAs show that there is virtually no differentiation in how the majority of FAs present
themselves to clients. If we put five FAs in separate elevators
and asked them to speak with a prospective client, all five
would say nearly the same thing. If the same client heard all
five elevator speeches, how would he begin to choose from
among them when all the alternatives seem the same? As

Figure A.10 List the Three Most Important Ways in Which Prospects Learn about You and Your Team's Products and Service Offerings

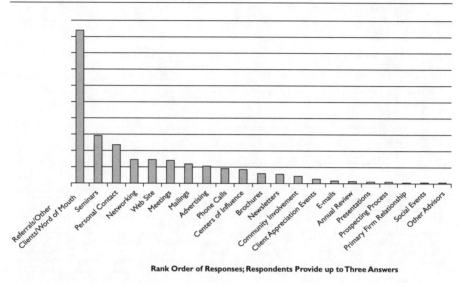

Rank Order of Responses; Respondents Provide up to Three Answers

a result, these attributes, as worthy as they are, essentially become table stakes. Without them, you can't get a seat at the table. Everyone has to have them, but they don't set you apart from the competition. In Chapters 4 and 9 we discuss this further and offer advice for moving beyond the most common attributes and instead generating your own list of three words that truly express how you are uniquely relevant to clients in your target segment.

Our survey results show that by far the most frequent way in which prospective clients learn about an FA's business is through referrals or word of mouth. As you can see in Figure A.10, word of mouth is mentioned more than three times as often as the next most common answers, which are seminars and direct personal contact from the FA. This is

Figure A.11 What Specific Tactics Do You Use to Encourage Referrals (Word of Mouth)?

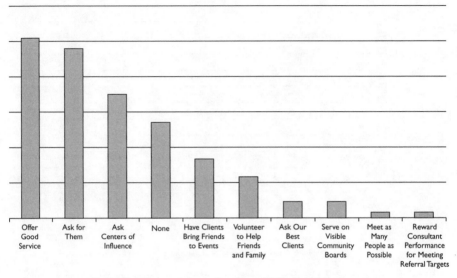

Offer Good Service | Ask for Them | Ask Centers of Influence | None | Have Clients Bring Friends to Events | Volunteer to Help Friends and Family | Ask Our Best Clients | Serve on Visible Community Boards | Meet as Many People as Possible | Reward Consultant Performance for Meeting Referral Targets

Rank Order of Responses; Respondents Allowed to List Multiple Tactics

not surprising. What is more surprising is how passive and nonstrategic many FAs are when it comes to trying to build word of mouth about their practices, as shown in Figure A.11. As we discuss throughout the book, referrals are the most credible source that leads to the greatest conversion of potential clients to clients.

When we ask FAs what specific actions, if any, they take to encourage or amplify word of mouth about their practice, most say that they encourage it by providing good service to their clients. Good service is clearly important, as clients are not going to tell other people how happy they are with your service if you are not providing good service. However, providing good service is not a *strategy* for encouraging word of mouth. The next most common answer to how FAs are encouraging word of mouth is simply "asking for it," either from clients or from centers of influence. What is clear is that a good number of respondents do nothing at all. Given the importance of word of mouth in every FA's business, developing a strategy to encourage it and shape it is critical, as we discuss in more detail in Chapter 8.

Not only should you be encouraging clients and collaborators to spread positive word of mouth about your practice, but you should also help them (and yourself) by making it easier for them to deliver that word of mouth to the right prospects and making sure that they are saying the right things. You want them to spread positive word of mouth to potential clients whom you can serve well and who will be valuable to you. Don't just ask for referrals. Ask for referrals to the right people. Make sure your clients know what characterizes your target market. Tell them that the clients you serve best are those who, like themselves, have certain characteristics. Be specific about those characteristics.

Once your clients know whom to talk to, make sure they know what to say. If they promise something that you cannot deliver, they are not doing you any favors. You cannot control what they say, but you can influence it. Make sure they know how you are differentiating yourself and your three words (Chapter 4). Make sure they can pass along your Web site address so that the prospective client can learn more for herself.

While you may want to encourage all of your existing clients to spread word of mouth, you may want to encourage it more from certain clients or collaborators than from others. You can see in the responses to our question that some FAs say they ask only their "best clients" for referrals. Some people are naturally better than others at spreading word of mouth. Take a look at your client list. Are there certain clients who have made successful referrals in the past? Note that this suggests keeping track of this information, something that we discuss in detail in Chapter 7. Make sure you are encouraging future referrals especially from those clients.

You'll also notice that some FAs say that they encourage word of mouth by serving on visible community boards. This is a terrific strategy. In their book *The Influentials*,[1] authors Jon Berry and Ed Keller distill decades' worth of research at Roper Polls into who spreads worth of mouth. In the book, they suggest that certain individuals are more likely to pass along word of mouth than others. These "influentials," for example, have a broader network of contacts, partly because they are more likely to be active in community associations and activities. Even in their leisure time, they are more likely to include other people in their plans, rather than engaging in activities alone or just with their immediate families. Individuals who are active in their communities are more likely to spread word of mouth. The more you are engaged with those "influentials," the more likely they are to be able to talk about you to others.

We ask our financial advisor respondents to tell us what they spend most of their time doing and then what they believe is actually most important to the success of their practices (see Figures A.12 and A.13). What you will notice is that most advisors rank marketing their products and services to their clients as something that they spend little time doing and as least important, among the offered alternatives,

Figure A.12 Please Rank the Following Items in Terms of How Much Time per Week (on Average) You Spend on Each Activity

Ranking of Amount of Time Spent	Activity
5 (Most Amount of Time)	Providing Service to Your Clients
4	Building a Relationship with Your Clients
3	Providing Advice to Your Clients
2	Providing Good Investment Performance to Your Clients
1 (Least Amount of Time)	Marketing Your Services or Products to Your Clients

Figure A.13 Please Rank the Following Items in Terms of How Important Each Is for the Success of Your Practice

Ranking of Importance	Activity
5 (Most Important)	Building a Relationship with Your Clients
4	Providing Service to Your Clients
3	Providing Advice to Your Clients
2	Providing Good Investment Performance to Your Clients
1 (Least Important)	Marketing Your Services or Products to Your Clients

to their business success. When we dig a little bit more, they will often say things like, "I don't spend time on marketing. Marketing isn't important to my business." Many FAs think that marketing is not necessary, and they underinvest in it. They equate selling with marketing. Well, we agree that selling products and services is probably less important than the other items on the list, but we disagree that marketing is not worth spending time on.

These questions are a bit of a red herring because, as we have argued, all of these things are marketing. In fact, we would argue that building relationships with clients and providing service to clients, the activities that are ranked as taking the most time and as the most important, *are* marketing. Satisfying the needs of your clients *is* marketing. Most FAs are doing marketing all the time, but they are doing it in an ad hoc, tactical way. All of these things should be integrated and should be vital to your overall marketing strategy. This book is all about developing a strategy and putting that strategy into practice so that it guides which clients you build relationships with, how you build those relationships, and how you provide service to those chosen clients over time. You are already a marketer. This book provides the tools to help you become a more focused, efficient, and effective marketer.

NOTE

1. Jon Berry and Ed Keller, *The Influentials: One American in Ten Tells the Other Nine How to Vote, Where to Eat, and What to Buy* (New York: Free Press, 2003).

REFERENCES

Belch, George, and Michael Belch. *Advertising and Promotion: An Integrated Marketing Communications Perspective.* New York: McGraw-Hill, 2009.

Berger, Paul D., and Nada I. Nasr. "Customer Lifetime Value: Marketing Models and Applications." *Journal of Interactive Marketing* 12, no. 1 (1998), 17–30.

Berry, Jon, and Ed Keller. *The Influentials: One American in Ten Tells the Other Nine How to Vote, Where to Eat and What to Buy.* New York: Free Press, 2003.

Heath, Chip, and Dan Heath. *Made to Stick: Why Some Ideas Survive and Others Die.* New York: Random House, 2007.

Keller, Kevin Lane. "Conceptualizing, Measuring and Managing Customer-Based Brand Equity." *Journal of Marketing* 57, no. 1 (January 1993), 1–22.

Keller, Kevin Lane. *Strategic Brand Management.* Upper Saddle River, N.J.: Prentice Hall, 1998.

Lodish, Leonard M., Ellen Curtis, Michael Ness, and M. Kerry Simpson. "Sales Force Sizing and Deployment Using a Decision Calculus Model at Syntex Laboratories." *Interfaces* 18, no. 1 (January-February 1988), 5–20.

Treacy, Michael, and Fred Wiersema. *The Discipline of Market Leaders: Choose Your Customers, Narrow Your Focus, Dominate Your Market.* New York: Basic Books, 1997.

ACKNOWLEDGMENTS

We would like to acknowledge all the financial advisors who have attended our classes at the Wharton School. The time we spent with all of you is what inspired us to write this book. We would also like to thank everyone at the Aresty Institute of Executive Education and the marketing department at the Wharton School, University of Pennsylvania. Additional thanks go to Leah Spiro and Colin Kelley at McGraw-Hill, who were instrumental in taking the book from an idea to the finished product. Lastly, we would especially like to thank Adela Mou for all her hard work, including data analysis, research, and general support.

INDEX

Branding umbrella, 87–88
Brands and branding, 81–105
 associations, 84–89
 described, 82–91
 ladder of branding, 89–91
 marketing plan, 231
 path model for differentiation, 91–96
  client intimacy, 92, 93–94, 95
  operational excellence, 92, 93, 95
  performance superiority, 92–93, 95
 perception of, 84–85
 points of pain, 101–102
 and segmentation, 38–39
 SWOT analysis, 10
 "three words" to articulate, 103–104
 touchpoints, 97–102
 what it is, 26, 81–82
Business Insights, 200

Charity involvement and affinity building, 222–224
Chase momentum, 141–142
Choice, increased, investor psychology, 134–136
Churn rate (P_t), CLV, 178–180
Client-centric orientation, marketing plan/strategic structure, 1–6, 24–25, 120
Clients:
 affinity building, 220–225
 asking for referrals, 204
 bias (*See* Psychology and bias, of investors)
 brand differentiation and client intimacy, 92, 93–94, 95
 decisions by (*See* Decision making, by client)
 departing, and competition information collection, 12
 developing deep understanding of, 4
 firing, 176–177, 182–183
 as five C, 7–8
 key client list, marketing plan, 234–235
 lifetime value (*See* Customer lifetime value [CLV])
 marketing plan/strategic structuring, 7–8, 229, 231, 241–242
 psychology of (*See* Psychology and bias, of investors)

relationship management (*See* Quantitative client relationship management [CRM])
 segmentation (*See* Segmentation)
"CNBC effect," 132–133, 138
Coca-Cola, 196
"Coffee can accounting," 158–161, 162
Cogent Research, 67, 127, 138
Collaborators, marketing plan/strategic structuring, 15–16, 229, 241–242
Columbia University, choice studies, 134–135
Communication (*See* Integrated marketing communication [IMC])
Community involvement and affinity building, 222–224
Company, marketing plan/strategic structuring, 9–10, 229, 241–242
Compatibility of resources, segmentation as, 47–48
Competition, marketing plan/strategic structuring, 10–13, 229, 241–242
Competitive set, marketing plan, 235
Complexity, investor psychology and bias, 132–136, 161
Concise marketing plan, 230, 233–236
Confidence, investor, 137–139
Consideration set, 83, 116–117
Consistency of marketing plan, 231
Content retirees, 72–73
Context:
 investor psychology and bias, 132–136, 161
 marketing plan/strategic structuring, 13–15, 229, 241–242
Contextual framework, marketing plan, 234
Continuer retirees, 74
Control, need for, 112–113
Cost of acquisition (C_0), CLV, 171, 174–175, 177–178
Cost of financial services (*See* Price)
Cost of marketing, x–xi, xv–xvii, 240–241
Costco, 95–96
Cs (*See* Five Cs)
Cultural groups, as niche sector, 65–66, 77–78
Customer lifetime value (CLV), 170–184
 assets under management, 171, 172
 client mix, 184

ABOUT THE AUTHORS

Eric T. Bradlow is the K.P. Chao Professor of Marketing, Statistics, and Education at the Wharton School.

Keith E. Niedermeier is the Director of the Undergraduate Marketing Program at the Wharton School.

Patti Williams is an Associate Professor of Marketing at the Wharton School.